CAMI KOEPP

The Time Between Stars

This book was professionally typeset on Reedsy.
Find out more at reedsy.com

Contents

One

The Wrong Turn

Rain poured down in relentless sheets, drenching the streets of New York City. Emily Carter cursed under her breath as she clutched her camera bag tighter and sprinted toward the nearest awning. Her sneakers splashed in a puddle, sending cold water up her jeans. It was one of those days where the universe seemed determined to laugh at her.

Of all days, she muttered, her voice barely audible over the rumble of thunder.

She glanced at her watch. She had exactly ten minutes to get to the gallery, a seemingly impossible task given the weather and the fact that she had no idea where she was. Emily had a knack for taking wrong turns, both figuratively and literally, and today was no exception.

Determined, she ducked into an alleyway, her shortcut to salvation—or so she thought.

That was when she collided, full force, with what felt like a wall. A very human, very solid wall. Her camera bag hit the ground with a thud, followed by a muffled expletive from the man she'd just run into.

Oh, come on! Emily groaned, brushing wet strands of hair out of her face. Can this day get any worse?

The wall turned out to be a tall man with piercing blue eyes and a sharp jawline that could've been chiseled by the gods themselves. He was dressed in a tailored gray suit, now speckled with rain and what looked suspiciously like coffee. His dark hair clung to his forehead, and his expression was a mix of irritation and disbelief.

You've got to be kidding me, he said, inspecting the damage to his suit. His voice was deep, velvety, and filled with disdain. Do you even look where you're going?

Do you? Emily shot back, scooping up her bag. You're the one standing in the middle of an alley like some sort of human roadblock.

I was walking to my car, he said, gesturing to a sleek black sedan parked a few feet away. Not loitering. There's a difference.

Well, congratulations. Your car looks just as miserable as the rest of us in this weather, Emily snapped. Now, if you'll excuse me, I have somewhere to be.

He raised an eyebrow, clearly unimpressed. With an attitude like that, I can't imagine anywhere that's expecting you.

Emily opened her mouth to retort, but a loud clap of thunder cut her off. She glanced at her watch again. Five minutes. No time for verbal sparring.

Goodbye, Mr. Grumpy, she said, sidestepping him and making a mad dash toward the street.

Miss Oblivious, he muttered under his breath, shaking his head as he climbed into his car.

Emily arrived at the gallery just as the event was starting. She was soaked to the bone and looked more like a drowned rat than a professional photographer. As she stepped inside, she was greeted by a blast of warm air and the clinking of wine glasses.

The gallery buzzed with chatter. Sleek, modern photographs lined the walls, illuminated by soft, flattering lights. Emily's stomach flipped. This wasn't just any exhibition—this was the exhibition. An opportunity to showcase her work and maybe, just maybe, catch the attention of someone important. She straightened her damp blazer and forced a smile.

Emily! her friend and gallery curator, Sasha, waved her over. You made it! Barely.

Long story, Emily said, rolling her eyes. Let's just say the universe and I aren't on speaking terms today.

Cheer up, Sasha said, handing her a glass of champagne. You're about to mingle with some serious talent. Oh, and we have a special guest speaker tonight. You'll love him.

Emily raised an eyebrow. Who?

Before Sasha could answer, the sound of a microphone crackling to life silenced the room. Emily turned toward the small stage at the front of the gallery—and nearly dropped her champagne.

There, standing under the spotlight, was none other than Mr. Grumpy himself.

Michael Blake adjusted the microphone stand and cleared his throat. He looked polished, confident, and completely unfazed by the storm outside.

Good evening, he began, his voice calm and commanding. Tonight, I want to talk about the intersection of art and science—specifically, how the cosmos can inspire creativity.

Emily blinked, certain she was hallucinating. Of all the people in New York City, how was he here?

She tried to blend into the crowd, but Michael's gaze swept across the room—and landed squarely on her. For a split second, his expression flickered with recognition. Then, to her horror, the faintest smirk curved his lips.

As I was saying, he continued, the universe has a way of connecting people in the most unexpected ways.

Emily clenched her jaw. Oh, he was enjoying this.

After the speech, the crowd dispersed into smaller groups, and Emily did her best to avoid Michael. But fate, as usual, had other plans.

Miss Oblivious, came a familiar voice behind her.

She turned to find Michael standing there, arms crossed, his smirk firmly in place.

It's Emily, she said, narrowing her eyes. And what are you doing here?

I could ask you the same thing, he replied. But since I'm the guest speaker, I think I have the upper hand.

Congratulations, Emily said flatly. You win the award for Most Annoying Person I've Met Today.

Michael chuckled. And you win for Least Gracious. Is this how you treat everyone you run into? Literally?

Emily sighed, deciding she didn't have the energy for another argument. Look, I'm sorry for earlier. It was a bad day.

Michael tilted his head, as if studying her. Apology accepted. But you might want to work on your navigational skills.

Emily rolled her eyes. Duly noted. Now, if you'll excuse me—

Wait, Michael said, surprising her. His tone softened. Your photography. It's good. Really good.

Emily blinked, caught off guard. You've seen it?

I make it a point to research the exhibitions I speak at, he said simply. Your work stood out.

Before she could respond, Sasha called her name from across the room. Emily hesitated, then turned to leave.

See you around, Miss Obliv—Emily, Michael called after her.

Emily didn't look back, but she couldn't stop the small smile that crept onto her face.

Back at her apartment, Emily opened her bag to retrieve her camera. Nestled inside, she found a folded note she didn't remember putting there. It read:

Sometimes, the wrong turn leads to the right place.

Two

A Sky Full of Secrets

The note sat on Emily's coffee table, mocking her with its cryptic message. She had read it a dozen times since finding it tucked into her camera bag. There was no name, no clue as to who had written it. Just those twelve infuriatingly vague words:

Sometimes, the wrong turn leads to the right place.

She tried to shake it off, chalking it up to some well-meaning stranger at the gallery. But deep down, she had a sneaking suspicion that he—Mr. Grumpy, aka Michael Blake—might have had something to do with it. The thought annoyed her as much as it intrigued her.

Stop obsessing, Emily, she muttered, flopping onto her couch. He's just a stuck-up astronomer with a superiority complex. Nothing more.

Still, she couldn't shake the memory of his speech. There had been a passion in his voice when he spoke about the cosmos—a reverence that had stirred something in her. It was rare for someone to talk about their work with such unguarded awe.

The next evening, Sasha roped Emily into attending another event at the gallery. This one was smaller, more intimate—a networking mixer for the artists and contributors. Emily had planned to decline, but Sasha had that way of guilt-tripping her that only best friends could master.

Think of it as a chance to meet potential clients, Sasha had insisted. And, who knows? Maybe Mr. Grumpy will be there.

Emily had rolled her eyes. Please don't call him that in public.

Why not? It fits him perfectly, Sasha teased, nudging Emily with her elbow.

Emily sighed but didn't argue. The truth was, she hadn't stopped thinking about Michael since the gallery speech—or the mysterious note. But she wasn't about to admit that to Sasha.

The gallery buzzed with quiet chatter as Emily scanned the room. It was filled with the usual crowd art enthusiasts, fellow photographers, and a few high-profile guests Sasha had somehow managed to lure in.

And then she saw him.

Michael Blake stood near the corner of the room, looking infuriatingly composed in a charcoal-gray blazer. He was deep in conversation with an older man who looked just as distinguished. Emily's heart did an odd little flip, which she quickly tried to squash.

Speak of the devil, Sasha whispered, following her gaze. You should go talk to him.

What? No way. Emily shook her head vehemently. I'm here to network, not to… whatever that would be.

Suit yourself, Sasha said with a shrug. But you know what they say about the wrong turn leading to the right place…

Emily glared at her. You've been reading my notes?

What? No! Sasha looked genuinely offended. Wait, what note?

Never mind. Emily waved her off, determined not to let Michael—or Sasha's meddling—consume her evening.

But, as fate would have it, avoiding Michael proved impossible.

As Emily perused a wall of black-and-white portraits, a low, familiar voice interrupted her thoughts.

Do you always scowl when you look at art, or is this a special occasion?

Emily turned to find Michael standing beside her, his hands casually in his pockets. He wore that same maddening smirk that made her want to both slap and kiss him—a confusing combination she wasn't eager to unpack.

Only when I've been ambushed, she retorted.

Michael chuckled, tilting his head toward the photograph she'd been staring at. What do you think of this one?

Emily crossed her arms. It's fine. A little predictable, maybe. But technically solid.

Michael raised an eyebrow. Harsh critic, are we?

Honest critic, she corrected. And what about you, Mr. Cosmos? Do you stare at art and try to calculate its place in the universe?

Not quite, he said, his tone lighter than she'd expected. But I do think art and science have more in common than most people realize.

Let me guess, Emily said, narrowing her eyes. You're about to make some profound analogy about stars and photography.

Michael grinned. I could, but I'd rather not waste it on someone who's already made up her mind about me.

Emily opened her mouth to reply, but Michael beat her to it.

You know, your work really did stand out, he said, his voice softening. It's not just technically impressive—it's personal. You capture moments that feel… alive.

Emily blinked, taken aback. She wasn't used to compliments, especially ones so specific. Thank you, she said cautiously. That's… actually nice of you to say.

Don't get used to it, Michael said with a teasing glint in his eye. I'm only nice on Tuesdays.

Emily couldn't help but laugh. Against her better judgment, she was beginning to find his dry humor oddly charming.

The night wore on, and Emily found herself drawn into a surprisingly easy conversation with Michael. They debated art versus science, shared stories about their work, and even bonded over a mutual hatred of pretentious party snacks.

But then, just as she was starting to let her guard down, Michael's demeanor shifted. His gaze grew distant, and his jaw tightened, as if he were suddenly somewhere else entirely.

Are you okay? Emily asked, her voice laced with genuine concern.

Michael hesitated, then forced a small smile. Yeah. Just a lot on my mind.

Before Emily could press further, Sasha appeared at her side, breathless and wide-eyed.

Emily, you have to see this, Sasha said, tugging her away from Michael.

What is it? Emily asked, glancing back at Michael, who now looked even more distracted.

Sasha handed her a magazine, the gallery's promotional brochure for the month. Emily's breath caught when she saw the featured article:

The Cosmos Within Us An Exclusive Interview with Michael Blake.

Why are you showing me this? Emily asked, confused.

Read the pull quote, Sasha urged, pointing to a bold line in the middle of the page.

Emily read it aloud:

'The universe is full of secrets, and sometimes, those secrets find you when you least expect them.'

Her heart skipped a beat. Those words sounded eerily similar to the note she'd found.

Do you think— Emily began, but when she looked up, Michael was gone.

Later that night, Emily sat alone in her apartment, staring at the note again.

The coincidence was too strange to ignore. Could Michael have written it? And if so, why?

Before she could overthink it further, her phone buzzed with a text. It was from Sasha

Guess who's a regular guest speaker at the Hayden Planetarium? You should go. ;)

Emily groaned. The last thing she wanted was to walk into Michael's orbit again. But something about his words, both at the gallery and in that interview, had hooked her.

The universe is full of secrets…

She glanced at her camera bag, then at the note. Maybe, just maybe, she'd take Sasha's advice.

As Emily debated her next move, another text came in—from an unknown number. It read:

The answers you're looking for are written in the stars.

Three

Coffee, Chaos, and Chemistry

The next morning, Emily groggily stared at her phone, the mysterious text still glaring back at her: *The answers you're looking for are written in the stars.*

The logical side of her screamed to ignore it—probably some prank or spam message. But the tiny, reckless part of her, the part that had once convinced her to dye her hair blue on a whim, whispered, What if it's not?

Sasha's suggestion about the Hayden Planetarium gnawed at her. Maybe Michael Blake was more than a smug astronomer with a penchant for cryptic one-liners. Maybe he held the key to… something. She wasn't sure what, but her curiosity was winning out.

Fine, she muttered, tossing her phone onto her bed. I'll go. Worst-case scenario, I leave halfway through and grab a latte.

The Hayden Planetarium was a world apart from Emily's usual haunts. She felt out of place among the families, tourists, and the occasional overenthusiastic science nerd wearing a galaxy-printed hoodie. Still, she managed to slip into the auditorium unnoticed, finding a seat in the back.

The room dimmed, and Michael stepped onto the stage. His commanding presence was impossible to ignore.

Welcome, he began, his voice calm yet magnetic. Today, we're exploring the concept of time—how it warps, bends, and connects us in ways we can't always see.

Emily settled into her seat, drawn in despite herself. He spoke about distant stars, gravitational waves, and the paradox of time itself, weaving science with something deeper—almost poetic. It was oddly mesmerizing.

But just as Emily was beginning to relax, Michael's gaze swept over the audience. For a fleeting moment, their eyes locked. He faltered, his words catching for a fraction of a second before he recovered. Emily's stomach did a somersault.

After the lecture, the audience filtered out, leaving Emily sitting frozen in her seat. Her heart raced as she debated her next move. Should she just leave and pretend she hadn't come? Or should she confront him about the text, the note, and everything else that had been gnawing at her since their first encounter?

Before she could decide, Michael appeared at the edge of the stage, scanning the room. His sharp blue eyes locked onto hers again, and this time there was no mistaking it—he was looking for her.

Well, you're either my biggest fan, or you're here to heckle me, Michael said as he approached, a teasing lilt in his voice.

Emily stood, clutching her bag like a lifeline. I'm still deciding, she replied, raising an eyebrow. Your lecture wasn't bad, though. A bit dramatic, but not bad.

Michael chuckled, shoving his hands into his pockets. I'll take that as a compliment. What brings you here? Interested in the secrets of the universe?

Something like that. Emily hesitated, then blurted out, Did you send me a text?

Michael frowned, genuinely puzzled. A text?

Yeah. It said, 'The answers you're looking for are written in the stars.' Ring any bells?

His confusion seemed genuine, but then his lips twitched into a small smile. Sounds like something I'd say, but no, it wasn't me. Should I be flattered you thought it was?

Emily groaned. Of course not. It was just… weird timing.

Michael tilted his head, studying her. Weird timing seems to be our specialty.

Great. Just what I needed—an astrophysical stalker, Emily muttered, mostly to herself.

Michael laughed, a sound surprisingly warm and unguarded. Don't worry, I'm too busy stalking black holes to bother with humans.

Emily's lips quirked despite herself. Well, Mr. Cosmos, as fun as this is, I should go.

Wait. Michael's tone shifted, softer now. Do you have time for coffee? I promise no more lectures.

Emily blinked, caught off guard. She opened her mouth to refuse, but curiosity got the better of her. Fine. But if you start talking about wormholes,

I'm leaving.

The coffee shop Michael chose was tucked into a quiet corner of the city, its walls adorned with quirky constellations and mismatched chairs. It felt intimate, almost too intimate, but Emily decided to roll with it.

They ordered their drinks—black coffee for Michael, a caramel latte for Emily—and settled into a small corner table. For a moment, neither of them spoke, the silence stretching awkwardly.

So, Michael finally said, leaning back in his chair. Why photography?

Emily sipped her latte, grateful for the distraction. Why not? It's how I make sense of the world. I can capture a moment, freeze it in time, and make it mean something.

Michael nodded thoughtfully. Sounds like you're bending time in your own way.

Don't try to turn this into one of your science metaphors, Emily warned, but her tone was light.

I wouldn't dream of it, Michael said, though the corner of his mouth twitched. What's your favorite photo you've ever taken?

Emily hesitated, caught off guard by the sincerity of his question. It's one I took of my dad, she admitted. We were at this old train station. He was laughing at something, and I caught it mid-laugh. It's… him, you know? Completely him.

Michael's expression softened. Sounds like a good memory.

It is. Emily stared into her cup, a lump forming in her throat. He passed away a few years ago.

I'm sorry, Michael said, his voice low.

Emily shrugged, though the pain still lingered. It's okay. Photography keeps him close. He used to love looking at the stars, actually. I think he would've liked you.

Michael smiled, his gaze distant. The stars have a way of connecting people.

Emily's heart skipped a beat. There it was again—that strange feeling, like he was speaking in riddles she was meant to solve. You're full of cryptic lines, aren't you?

Michael chuckled. Occupational hazard.

They talked until their cups were empty, the conversation surprisingly easy. Emily found herself laughing more than she'd expected, drawn to Michael's dry humor and subtle charm. He wasn't as aloof as she'd thought—there was a depth to him, a quiet intensity that intrigued her.

But just as the moment began to feel almost too comfortable, Michael glanced at his watch and stood abruptly.

I should go, he said, his tone suddenly guarded. I have a meeting.

Right, Emily said, trying to hide her disappointment. Well, thanks for the coffee. And the… stargazing tips, or whatever.

Michael hesitated, as if he wanted to say something else. But instead, he pulled a small notebook from his jacket pocket, scribbled something on a page, and handed it to her.

Here, he said. If you ever want to learn more about the stars.

Emily frowned, unfolding the note as he walked away. Written in neat, precise handwriting was an address. No explanation, no instructions—just an address.

Emily debated throwing the note away but couldn't shake the feeling that Michael was leading her toward something important. That night, curiosity won. She typed the address into her phone's GPS, and her heart raced as she realized where it led the observatory.

Four

A Timeless Photograph

Emily stood outside the observatory, clutching the note Michael had given her. The massive structure loomed above her, its dome glowing faintly under the night sky. She hadn't intended to come this far, but something about the address—and Michael's enigmatic demeanor—had pulled her here.

Why do I let myself get dragged into this nonsense? she muttered, pulling her jacket tighter around her.

Inside, the observatory was dimly lit, its walls lined with posters of galaxies, nebulae, and swirling constellations. The air smelled faintly of metal and something sharp, like freshly cleaned glass. It was eerily quiet, and Emily felt like she had stepped into another world.

A receptionist glanced up from the desk. Can I help you?

Emily hesitated, feeling suddenly self-conscious. Uh, I think I'm supposed to meet Michael Blake?

The receptionist smiled knowingly. Dr. Blake is in the main observatory.

Take the stairs up to the dome.

Thanks, Emily said, her stomach twisting as she climbed the stairs.

The dome was breathtaking. The ceiling opened up to reveal the night sky in all its splendor, stars glittering like scattered diamonds. In the center of the room, Michael stood beside a massive telescope, his back to her.

Nice place, Emily said, her voice echoing slightly.

Michael turned, startled, but his expression softened when he saw her. You came.

Against my better judgment, she quipped, crossing her arms. So, what's this all about? You hand me a cryptic note, send me to the middle of nowhere, and now… what? We stare at stars?

Michael smirked, gesturing toward the telescope. Something like that. Come here.

Emily hesitated but walked over. He adjusted the telescope and stepped aside, motioning for her to look. Go on. Take a peek.

She leaned in, the cold metal pressing against her forehead. Through the lens, she saw a dazzling cluster of stars, their light shimmering as if they were alive. It was beautiful, almost overwhelming.

Wow, she whispered. That's… incredible.

Orion Nebula, Michael said, his voice low. A birthplace of stars. It's been around for millions of years, but the light we're seeing now is only just reaching us.

Emily pulled back, her brow furrowing. So, we're basically looking into the past?

Exactly. Michael leaned against the railing, his gaze fixed on the sky. The stars remind us that time isn't as straightforward as we think. The past, present, and future are all connected.

Emily tilted her head. Is this your way of saying I should stop procrastinating?

Michael chuckled. Not exactly. But maybe you should think about how the past shapes who we are.

The way he said it made Emily pause. There was something in his tone—something heavy, almost sad. She wanted to ask what he meant, but before she could, Michael gestured toward a small table in the corner.

I found something I thought you might want to see, he said, his voice quieter now.

Curious, Emily followed him. On the table was a stack of old photographs. Michael handed her one, his expression unreadable.

Emily froze when she saw the image. It was an old, faded photograph of a man standing in front of a telescope. He was laughing, his eyes crinkled with joy.

Her father.

Where did you get this? she asked, her voice barely above a whisper.

It was in the observatory's archives, Michael said. I recognized your name from the gallery and made the connection. Your father worked on a project here years ago—before I started.

Emily stared at the photo, her mind reeling. Her father had never mentioned anything about working at an observatory. Photography had always been his passion, or so she'd thought.

This doesn't make any sense, she murmured. Why wouldn't he tell me about this?

Michael hesitated, then said, There's more.

He handed her a second photograph. This one showed a group of scientists standing together, smiling proudly. Among them was her father—and a much younger Michael.

Emily's jaw dropped. You… you knew him?

Michael nodded, his expression somber. I was an intern here at the time. Your father was one of the kindest, most brilliant people I'd ever met. He inspired me to pursue astronomy.

Emily couldn't process what she was hearing. Why didn't you say anything before?

I didn't want to overwhelm you, Michael said. And honestly, I wasn't sure it was the same man until I found this.

He handed her a small notebook, its leather cover worn and cracked. When Emily opened it, she recognized her father's handwriting immediately. Inside were sketches of constellations, notes about the stars, and a few entries that hinted at something deeper—a project he had been working on, one he had called: **The Time Between Stars.**

What is this? she asked, her voice trembling.

Michael shook his head. I don't know. But it seems important.

The room felt heavier now, as if the stars above them were pressing down on her. Emily clutched the notebook tightly, her mind swirling with questions. Why had her father kept this part of his life a secret? What was The Time Between Stars, and why did Michael seem so invested in it?

Before she could say anything, Michael's phone buzzed. He glanced at the screen, his expression darkening.

I have to go, he said abruptly, already moving toward the stairs.

What? Now? Emily called after him. We're in the middle of something!

I'll explain later, Michael said, his voice tense. Stay as long as you want. Just… be careful with that notebook.

And with that, he was gone, leaving Emily alone under the stars.

Emily flipped through the notebook again, stopping on a page where her father had written in bold letters, **The universe doesn't give us answers—it gives us questions.** Beneath it was a sketch of the Orion Nebula… and a name she didn't recognize. Michael's father.

Five

Stuck Between Stars

Emily sat in the observatory under the vast dome of stars, her father's notebook open on her lap. Her fingers traced the bold handwriting where he had scrawled the name *Michael's father.*

What is this? she murmured to herself, flipping through the rest of the pages. Sketches of constellations, complex equations, and cryptic notes filled the small notebook, but nothing else explicitly mentioned Michael or his family. Yet, the name leapt off the page, refusing to be ignored.

The sound of distant footsteps startled her, and Emily quickly tucked the notebook into her bag. She glanced around, half-expecting Michael to return, but the observatory was empty. Still, a chill crept up her spine.

Why did he leave so suddenly? she thought. The intensity on his face as he walked out wasn't just urgency—it was fear.

The next day, Emily couldn't focus on anything else. She stared at her laptop, the cursor blinking mockingly in the middle of an unfinished email. She had deadlines to meet, edits to make, and a list of mundane chores she'd been avoiding, but her mind kept drifting back to the notebook and the question it raised.

Finally, she gave in. She grabbed her phone and dialed Sasha.

Hey, what's up? Sasha answered, her voice cheerful. You sound like you're about to ask me for a favor.

That's because I am, Emily said, pacing her small apartment. How do I find information about someone from, like, twenty years ago? Specifically, someone connected to an observatory?

Sasha let out a low whistle. Getting into the mystery-solving business now, are we?

Let's just say I've stumbled onto something… weird. Can you help or not?

Lucky for you, I've got a friend at the public records office. Give me a name, and I'll see what I can dig up.

Emily hesitated before saying, Michael's father. That's all I've got. And… maybe check connections to the Hayden Planetarium.

Got it. I'll call you back, Sasha said before hanging up.

Emily exhaled, her stomach twisting. She didn't know what she was expecting to find, but the idea of uncovering more about Michael—or her father—both excited and terrified her.

Hours passed with no word from Sasha. Emily tried to distract herself by editing photos, but she couldn't focus. Just as she was about to call Sasha again, her phone buzzed.

Finally, she muttered, answering immediately. What did you find?

Emily… Sasha's voice was unusually serious. This is… strange. There's almost nothing about Michael Blake's father. No public records, no employment history. It's like the guy didn't exist.

Emily frowned. That doesn't make sense. He had to have worked at the observatory.

There's one thing, Sasha added. I found an old article in an academic journal. It mentions a Dr. Charles Blake—a physicist who worked on a project called The Time Between Stars. But get this the article was co-authored by your father.

Emily's breath caught. What?

Yeah. It's dated twenty-five years ago. The article doesn't give much detail, but it describes the project as a 'revolutionary exploration of time and space.' Then it cuts off.

Cuts off? Emily echoed. Like it's incomplete?

More like someone wanted it buried, Sasha said. It's weird, right?

Weird didn't even begin to cover it. Emily's mind raced. Her father and Michael's father had worked together on a secretive project—one that shared the same name as her father's notebook. But why hadn't she ever heard of it? And why had Michael avoided mentioning his family?

Sasha, can you send me the article? Emily asked, her voice tight.

Already did. Check your email. And Emily… be careful, okay? This feels bigger than it looks.

Thanks, Sasha, Emily said before hanging up.

Later that night, Emily sat at her desk, the glow of her laptop illuminating the dark room. She opened the email from Sasha and clicked on the attachment. The article was dense, filled with scientific jargon that made her head spin, but one line stood out

The Time Between Stars aims to bridge the gap between past and future, proving that time is not a linear construct but a malleable dimension.

Emily leaned back in her chair, the weight of those words sinking in. If her father and Michael's father had been researching time itself, what had they found? And why had the project been abandoned?

She pulled out the notebook again, flipping to the pages with the equations. She didn't understand the math, but there was a pattern to the symbols—a rhythm that felt deliberate. It was as if her father had been trying to leave a message.

A loud knock at her door made her jump. Her heart pounded as she approached cautiously, half-expecting to find Michael. Instead, Lucas, her childhood friend and occasional thorn in her side, stood in the hallway, holding two cups of coffee and wearing his signature lopsided grin.

Lucas? Emily said, surprised. What are you doing here?

Saving you from whatever rabbit hole you've fallen into, he said, brushing past her into the apartment. You've been ignoring my texts.

Emily sighed, closing the door. I've been busy.

Yeah, I figured. Lucas plopped onto her couch, setting the coffees on the table. What's going on, Em? You look like you've seen a ghost.

She hesitated, debating whether to tell him the truth. Lucas was her oldest friend, but he also had a habit of prying too much. Still, she couldn't keep this to herself.

I think my dad was involved in something big, she finally said, sitting across from him. Like, bigger than photography. And I think Michael—this guy I've been… sort of getting to know—might be connected to it.

Lucas raised an eyebrow. Define 'getting to know.'

Emily rolled her eyes. Focus, Lucas. This is serious.

Okay, okay, he said, holding up his hands. What kind of 'big' are we talking about here? Government conspiracy? Time travel?

I don't know yet, Emily admitted. But it feels… important. Like my dad wanted me to find this.

Lucas studied her, his teasing demeanor replaced by quiet concern. You sure you're ready to dig into this? You don't know what you'll find.

Emily met his gaze, her resolve hardening. I have to know.

Just as Emily began to explain everything to Lucas, her phone buzzed. It was Michael. The message was short but chilling, *Don't trust anyone. Especially not me.*

Six

Gravity's Pull

Emily stared at the text, her heart hammering against her ribs. *Don't trust anyone. Especially not me.*

What's wrong? Lucas asked, leaning forward on the couch. You look like you've seen a ghost.

Emily quickly locked her phone, shoving it into her pocket. Nothing. It's nothing.

Don't give me that. Lucas narrowed his eyes. You're as subtle as a freight train, Em. What's going on?

She hesitated. Lucas was her oldest friend, the one person who had always been there for her. But Michael's warning reverberated in her mind, making her second-guess everything. Was Michael trying to protect her, or was he hiding something more sinister?

Just some… work stuff, she said finally, trying to sound casual. You know how it is.

Lucas didn't look convinced, but he didn't press. Okay. But if this mysterious work stuff turns out to be you getting mixed up in something dangerous, I'm going to start asking questions.

Emily forced a smile. Noted.

That night, sleep didn't come easily. Emily lay awake, staring at the ceiling, her father's notebook sitting on the nightstand like a beacon. Michael's text played on repeat in her mind. *Don't trust anyone. Especially not me.*

What was she supposed to make of that? Was he trying to warn her away, or was he dragging her deeper into whatever this was? And why had he even reached out to her in the first place if he thought she shouldn't trust him?

By the time the sun rose, Emily's restlessness had won. She threw on a sweatshirt, grabbed her bag, and headed to the coffee shop down the street, hoping a caffeine boost might bring some clarity.

The little café was bustling with its usual morning crowd, the hum of conversation and the hiss of the espresso machine filling the air. Emily placed her order—a large caramel latte—and found a quiet corner near the window to sit. As she waited for her drink, she pulled out the notebook, flipping through the pages again.

Every time she looked at it, new details seemed to emerge. Her father's handwriting, normally neat and controlled, was frantic in some sections, as though he'd been in a hurry to record his thoughts. The phrase - The Time Between Stars- appeared multiple times, accompanied by diagrams that made her head spin.

One page caught her attention. It wasn't filled with equations or sketches, but with a single, haunting sentence: *Time isn't a straight line—it's a web.*

What's got you so fascinated?

Emily nearly spilled her latte as Michael's voice broke through her thoughts. She looked up to find him standing beside her table, his expression unreadable.

What are you doing here? she asked, her voice sharper than she intended.

Michael slid into the seat across from her, ignoring the question. Couldn't sleep either?

Emily scowled. You don't get to just show up after sending me a text like that.

Michael leaned back in his chair, his gaze steady. And yet, here we are.

Care to explain what the hell you meant? she demanded, pulling out her phone and holding it up. Because telling someone not to trust you isn't exactly reassuring.

Michael sighed, running a hand through his hair. For the first time, he looked… tired. Vulnerable, even.

Look, he said, lowering his voice. You're not wrong to have questions. But the answers—whatever they are—might not be what you want to hear.

Emily leaned forward, her frustration bubbling over. Stop speaking in riddles, Michael. If you know something about my father or this project, just tell me.

Michael hesitated, glancing around the café as if checking for eavesdroppers. Then he leaned in closer, his voice barely above a whisper. Your father and my father weren't just colleagues. They were trying to prove something that most people would call impossible.

Prove what? Emily asked, her pulse quickening.

That time isn't fixed, Michael said, his eyes locking onto hers. That it's fluid. That under the right conditions, it can be… manipulated.

Emily's breath caught. The words sounded absurd, like something out of a science fiction novel. But the intensity in Michael's expression made her pause.

You're serious, she said, her voice barely audible.

Michael nodded. I didn't believe it at first, either. But the more I've looked into their work, the more I think they were onto something. And whatever they found… someone didn't want it to get out.

Emily's stomach twisted. What do you mean?

Michael hesitated, then said, My father disappeared shortly after the project was shut down. No explanation, no warning. Just… gone. Your father went quiet too, didn't he?

Emily nodded slowly. Her father had never talked about his work at the observatory, and now it made sense why. But one question still burned in her mind.

Why are you telling me this now? she asked.

Michael's expression darkened. Because whoever shut them down isn't done. And I think they're watching us.

Emily's head spun as she tried to process his words. The idea that her father had been involved in something so monumental—and so dangerous—felt impossible to grasp. And yet, a part of her had known from the moment she found the photograph that her life was about to change.

Before she could respond, the café door swung open, and Lucas walked in, spotting her immediately.

There you are, he said, striding over. Thought I'd find you here.

Michael tensed, his jaw tightening as Lucas approached. Emily glanced between the two of them, feeling the tension crackle in the air.

Lucas, what are you doing here? she asked.

Looking out for you, Lucas said, his gaze flicking to Michael. Who's this?

Michael stood, his posture rigid. Michael Blake.

Lucas's eyes narrowed. Right. The mysterious astrophysicist. Heard a lot about you.

Michael's expression remained calm, but his tone was icy. Likewise.

Emily groaned. Okay, can we not do this right now? Lucas, sit down. Michael, stop glaring.

Neither man moved.

Emily's phone buzzed, breaking the standoff. She glanced at the screen and froze. The message was short but chilling: *You're asking too many questions. Stop, or you'll regret it.*

Seven

Almost Confessions

The café seemed to grow colder as Emily stared at her phone, the words, *You're asking too many questions. Stop, or you'll regret it* glowing ominously on the screen. Her chest tightened, and for a moment, the noise of the bustling coffee shop faded into a dull hum.

Emily? Lucas's voice cut through the fog. What is it?

Emily quickly locked her phone and shoved it into her pocket. Nothing, she lied, her voice shaky. Just... work stuff.

Michael, who had been watching her closely, didn't look convinced. Was that another text? he asked, his tone sharp.

Emily glared at him, silently willing him not to press further. I said it's nothing.

Lucas frowned, his concern evident. You're terrible at lying, Em.

Drop it, she snapped, standing abruptly. The two men exchanged a tense glance, but neither pushed further.

I need some air, Emily muttered, grabbing her bag and heading for the door. She didn't look back to see if either of them followed.

Outside, the crisp morning air hit her like a slap, and Emily inhaled deeply, trying to steady her racing thoughts. Someone was watching her. Someone knew what she was digging into—and they didn't want her to continue.

Her fingers brushed against the edge of her father's notebook in her bag. She felt an overwhelming urge to protect it, to keep it close, as if it held the answers she so desperately needed.

The door to the café opened behind her, and Michael stepped out. His expression was serious, but there was a flicker of something else in his eyes—concern.

You're not okay, he said simply.

Emily crossed her arms, feeling exposed under his gaze. No kidding.

Michael took a step closer, lowering his voice. I don't mean to sound dramatic, but you need to take this seriously. If someone is trying to scare you off, it means you're getting close to something important.

And what if I don't want to be close to it? Emily shot back. I didn't ask for any of this, Michael. I just wanted to figure out why you gave me that stupid note in the first place!

Michael hesitated, then said, Because I think our fathers were trying to tell us something. Something that could change everything.

Emily's frustration flared. What does that even mean? Why can't you just give me a straight answer?

Michael ran a hand through his hair, clearly struggling with how much to reveal. Because I don't have all the answers, Emily. All I know is that our fathers were on the verge of something groundbreaking—and dangerous. And whatever they found… it's not just history. It's still happening.

Emily stared at him, her chest tight with a mix of anger and fear. Why didn't you tell me this sooner?

Michael's gaze softened. Because I didn't want to drag you into it. But now… it's too late.

Before Emily could respond, the door to the café swung open again, and Lucas stormed out. His expression was a mix of annoyance and worry.

Okay, what's going on? he demanded, looking between Emily and Michael. What are you two involved in?

Nothing, Emily said quickly, but Lucas wasn't buying it.

Don't give me that, Lucas snapped. You've been acting weird for days, and now you're sneaking around with this guy? What the hell is going on, Emily?

Michael's jaw tightened, but he stayed silent, letting Emily handle it.

It's complicated, she said, her voice weary. And it's not something I can explain right now.

Lucas's eyes narrowed. Not something you can explain, or not something you want to explain? Because from where I'm standing, it looks like this guy is dragging you into something dangerous.

Lucas, stop, Emily said, her voice sharper than she intended. You don't know what you're talking about.

Michael finally spoke, his tone calm but firm. Emily can make her own decisions. She doesn't need you to play bodyguard.

Oh, that's rich, Lucas shot back. Says the guy who clearly knows more than he's letting on.

Enough! Emily shouted, startling both men into silence. She took a shaky breath, trying to regain control. I don't have time for this right now. Both of you, just… back off.

She turned on her heel and walked away, ignoring their calls to come back.

Emily spent the rest of the day wandering the city, trying to make sense of everything. The text, the notebook, the article Sasha had sent her—it all pointed to something bigger than she could comprehend. But it also painted a target on her back.

By the time she returned to her apartment, the sun was setting, casting long shadows across the walls. She locked the door behind her and double-checked the windows, suddenly paranoid that someone might be watching.

Her phone buzzed again, and her stomach clenched. She half-expected another threatening message, but instead, it was an email from Sasha. The subject line read: Found Something Interesting.

Emily clicked it open, her heart racing. The email contained a scanned page from an old observatory report. One line stood out:

The Time Between Stars: Project suspended indefinitely due to unforeseen risks.

Beneath it was a handwritten note in the margin. It was her father's handwriting.

If you're reading this, trust Michael Blake. He's the only one who can help you.

Emily's breath caught. The message was clear—but it didn't make sense. If her father trusted Michael, why had Michael told her not to trust him? And what were these unforeseen risks that had shut down the project?

A loud knock at her door made her jump. She grabbed the notebook and clutched it to her chest, her heart pounding.

Who is it? she called, her voice trembling.

It's Lucas, came the muffled reply. We need to talk.

Emily hesitated, then opened the door. Lucas stood there, looking more serious than she'd ever seen him.

We're not alone in this, he said, stepping inside. I found something. And you're not going to like it.

Lucas pulled out a photograph and handed it to Emily. Her blood ran cold when she saw it. It was a picture of her father and Michael's father… standing with a group of people in military uniforms.

Eight

Echoes of the Past

Emily stared at the photograph Lucas had handed her, her mind racing. There was her father, younger but unmistakable, standing next to Michael's father, who bore an eerie resemblance to his son. They were surrounded by men in military uniforms, their expressions serious, almost foreboding. In the background, a massive telescope loomed, its structure half-hidden in shadow.

What is this? Emily asked, her voice barely above a whisper.

Lucas leaned against the doorframe, his usual easygoing demeanor replaced by a rare seriousness. I found it in the archives at the library. There's a whole section on government-funded observatory projects from the 90s. Your dad and Michael's dad weren't just working on some theoretical research. This was big—military big.

Emily's stomach twisted. Why would the military care about a project like The Time Between Stars?

Lucas shrugged, but his expression was grim. Time manipulation, maybe? Imagine if they could predict movements in space or even manipulate it for… I don't know, weapons or something. Whatever it was, it seems like they didn't want anyone to know about it.

She shook her head, the pieces of the puzzle refusing to fit together. But my dad wasn't the type to get involved in anything dangerous. He loved photography, not… this. She gestured at the photograph as though it could explain itself.

People can be full of surprises, Em, Lucas said gently. Maybe he didn't have a choice.

Emily sat down heavily on the couch, the photograph still clutched in her hands. Michael didn't mention anything about the military.

Of course he didn't, Lucas said, his voice sharp. How much do you actually know about him? He shows up out of nowhere, drops cryptic clues, and now you're mixed up in some secret project your dad worked on? Doesn't that seem a little too convenient?

Michael's not the enemy, Emily said defensively, though a part of her wondered if Lucas had a point.

Lucas crossed his arms. You sure about that?

The tension between them lingered as Emily studied the photograph. Something about it nagged at her, a detail she couldn't quite place. Then she saw it—the faint outline of a patch on one of the uniforms. It looked like a star surrounded by a ring, with the letters S.O.L.A.R. embroidered beneath it.

What's this? she asked, pointing at the patch.

Lucas leaned over to look. I noticed that too. I tried searching for anything related to 'SOLAR,' but I couldn't find much. Whatever it is, it's buried deep.

Emily frowned, tracing the outline of the patch with her finger. Michael might know.

Or he might give you another cryptic answer, Lucas muttered. Look, I get that you're curious about this guy, but don't forget who's got your back. I'm not going to let you walk into something dangerous just because he's good at brooding.

Emily shot him a look. Thanks for the vote of confidence.

Just being honest, Lucas said with a shrug. If you're really going to talk to him, at least take me with you.

I'll think about it, Emily said, though she wasn't sure if that was true.

Later that night, Emily sat in her apartment, the photograph and her father's notebook spread out on the coffee table. She couldn't shake the feeling that the answers were right in front of her, just out of reach.

Her phone buzzed, and she flinched, half-expecting another ominous text. Instead, it was Michael.

We need to talk. Can you meet me?

Emily hesitated, her thumb hovering over the screen. She still wasn't sure whether she could trust him, but if anyone knew what the patch meant—or what her father had been involved in—it was Michael.

Where? she texted back.

The reply came almost instantly. The rooftop at the Hayden Planetarium. Midnight.

The rooftop of the planetarium was eerily quiet when Emily arrived. The city stretched out below, a sea of glittering lights that seemed to echo the stars above. Michael stood near the edge, his silhouette framed by the glowing dome of the observatory. He turned as she approached, his expression unreadable.

You came, he said softly.

Couldn't resist the charm of a midnight meeting on a rooftop, Emily said, her voice tinged with sarcasm. But her heart was pounding, and she knew he could probably tell.

Michael gestured toward a bench, and they sat in tense silence for a moment before he spoke. You've been digging, haven't you?

Emily pulled the photograph from her bag and handed it to him. You tell me.

Michael's jaw tightened as he studied the image. Where did you get this?

Lucas found it in the library archives, Emily said. He thinks our dads were working on something for the military. Something called SOLAR. Sound familiar?

Michael exhaled slowly, his gaze still fixed on the photograph. My father mentioned SOLAR once. He said it was the funding body behind The Time Between Stars. But he never told me what it stood for.

Why didn't you tell me about the military connection? Emily pressed.

Because I didn't know for sure, Michael said, his voice edged with frustration. I've been trying to piece this together just like you have. But whoever shut this project down did a damn good job of erasing everything.

Emily studied him, trying to gauge whether he was being truthful. What about your father? Do you really think he just… disappeared?

Michael hesitated, then nodded. He left one day and never came back. No explanation, no note. Just gone. I used to think he abandoned us, but now… He trailed off, his expression darkening. Now I'm not so sure.

Emily swallowed hard, the weight of his words sinking in. Do you think my dad knew what was going to happen?

Michael glanced at her, his eyes filled with a quiet intensity. I think they both knew more than they let on. And I think they were trying to protect us.

From what? Emily whispered.

Michael looked up at the stars, his expression distant. That's what we need to figure out.

Just as the silence between them grew comfortable, Emily's phone buzzed again. She pulled it out and froze. The message was simple but chilling: *SOLAR isn't just watching. They're coming.*

Nine

The Day the Stars Collided

Emily's hands shook as she stared at the message on her phone: *SOLAR isn't just watching. They're coming.*

Michael, she whispered, her voice trembling. We have a problem.

Michael turned to her, his sharp blue eyes narrowing at the panic in her tone. What is it?

Wordlessly, she handed him the phone. His expression darkened as he read the text, his jaw clenching tightly. Whoever this is, they're escalating, he said, his voice low and controlled. We don't have much time.

Time for what? Emily asked, her heart racing. Michael, what's going on?

Michael stood abruptly, pacing the rooftop. SOLAR isn't just a funding body. If they're still active—and it looks like they are—then they're not here to answer questions. They're here to make sure we stop asking them.

Emily's stomach turned. Are you saying they're dangerous?

Michael stopped pacing and faced her, his expression grim. I'm saying they'll do whatever it takes to protect their secrets. Including silencing anyone who gets too close.

The weight of his words hit her like a punch to the gut. Her father's involvement, Michael's father's disappearance, the cryptic notebook—it all felt like pieces of a puzzle she didn't want to finish.

So what do we do? she asked, trying to keep her voice steady.

Michael glanced at the glowing dome of the observatory behind them, his mind clearly racing. We need to find out what your father and mine were really working on. If SOLAR's after us, it's because we're close to something they don't want us to know.

Emily hesitated, her fear clawing at the edges of her resolve. And how exactly do we do that without… you know, getting ourselves killed?

Michael's lips twitched into a humorless smile. Carefully.

By the time they left the planetarium, the city was quiet, the streets bathed in the eerie glow of streetlights. Michael insisted on walking her back to her apartment, his posture tense and alert as if expecting an ambush at any moment.

When they reached her building, Emily hesitated on the steps, clutching her bag tightly. Michael, she said softly, why are you still here? You could have walked away from all of this.

Michael's expression softened, a flicker of vulnerability breaking through his usual composure. Because your father saved my life once. And because I couldn't live with myself if I let you face this alone.

Emily's breath caught at the sincerity in his voice. What do you mean, he saved your life?

Michael glanced away, as if debating whether to tell her. It was years ago. I was just a kid, barely old enough to understand what my father was working on. There was an accident at the observatory—something went wrong with the equipment. Your dad pulled me out before things got worse.

She stared at him, her heart aching at the weight of his words. I didn't know.

You wouldn't have, Michael said quietly. Your dad was a good man. He didn't talk about himself much, did he?

Emily shook her head, a lump forming in her throat. No. He always seemed… distracted. Like there was something he wanted to tell me but couldn't.

Michael nodded, his gaze distant. Maybe he wanted to protect you from this.

Maybe, Emily whispered, though the thought brought little comfort.

When Emily finally went inside, she didn't sleep. Instead, she spread her father's notebook, the photograph, and Sasha's scanned article across her coffee table, trying to make sense of it all. Every clue pointed to The Time Between Stars as the key to understanding what SOLAR was trying to hide, but the details were maddeningly incomplete.

The name SOLAR stuck out like a beacon. Emily opened her laptop and began typing furiously, searching for any connection to the observatory, her father, or Michael's father. Most of what she found was useless—generic references to solar energy projects and astronomical studies. But then she stumbled across an obscure reference in an old physics journal:

SOLAR: Strategic Operations for Longitudinal Astronomical Research.

Founded in 1985 as a joint initiative between civilian scientists and military advisors.

Emily's stomach tightened as she read the next line: **The organization was disbanded in 1998 following classified investigations into its methodologies.**

Classified investigations? she murmured, her fingers hovering over the keyboard. What the hell were they doing?

Before she could dig further, a loud knock at her door made her jump. Her heart pounded as she approached cautiously, peering through the peephole. To her relief—and mild annoyance—it was Lucas.

She opened the door, crossing her arms. Lucas, it's late.

I know, he said, stepping inside uninvited. But I couldn't sleep. Something about that photo is bugging me.

Emily sighed, closing the door behind him. You and me both.

Lucas sat down on the couch, picking up the photograph. This patch, he said, pointing to the SOLAR emblem. It's military, sure, but it's not like any branch I've ever seen.

And? Emily prompted, sinking into the seat beside him.

And it means this isn't just some science experiment gone wrong, Lucas said, his tone grim. This was black ops. Top secret. The kind of thing people disappear over.

Emily shivered at his words. You're really not helping, you know.

I'm not trying to scare you, Lucas said gently. I just want you to be careful.

Whoever sent you that text… they're not playing around.

Emily opened her mouth to respond, but her phone buzzed again. Her stomach dropped as she saw the message:

You're running out of time. Leave it alone, or you'll lose everything.

Emily's hands trembled as she showed Lucas the text. His face hardened as he pulled out his phone and said, We're not waiting around anymore. We're going to find Michael—and we're getting to the bottom of this tonight.

Ten

Jealousy in the Air

Lucas drove them through the quiet city streets, his jaw clenched in concentration, his knuckles tight on the steering wheel. Emily sat beside him, clutching her bag as if it held all the answers she needed—her father's notebook, the photograph, and the growing storm of questions swirling in her mind.

Are we just going to show up at Michael's place and demand answers? Emily asked, breaking the silence.

That's the plan, Lucas said flatly.

What if he doesn't know anything else? Or worse, what if he's part of this?

Lucas glanced at her, his eyes sharp. If he's part of this, we'll find out soon enough.

Emily sighed, resting her head against the window. The city lights blurred as they passed, their glow a stark contrast to the dark unease gnawing at her. She didn't know if she could trust Michael, but she couldn't shake the feeling that he was somehow as caught up in this as she was.

When they arrived at Michael's building, Lucas parked haphazardly, and they climbed the stairs to his apartment. Emily hesitated outside his door, her hand hovering over the buzzer.

Ready? Lucas asked, his voice low.

Not even a little, Emily muttered, but she pressed the buzzer anyway.

For a moment, there was nothing. Then the intercom crackled, and Michael's voice came through, sounding wary. Who is it?

It's Emily, she said. And… Lucas.

There was a long pause before the door buzzed open. Emily exchanged a look with Lucas before they headed inside.

Michael opened the door to his apartment wearing a T-shirt and jeans, looking more casual than Emily had ever seen him. His usually guarded expression flickered with annoyance as his eyes landed on Lucas.

What's he doing here? Michael asked, his tone cold.

Lucas stepped forward, his shoulders squared. I'm here because I care about Emily and don't trust you.

Good to know, Michael said dryly, stepping aside to let them in. Make yourself comfortable—though I doubt that's possible for you.

Boys, can we not? Emily said, stepping between them. We have bigger problems right now.

Michael's apartment was minimalist and tidy, with bookshelves lined with astronomy texts and a sleek telescope by the window. Emily glanced at the city skyline visible through the glass before turning back to Michael.

I got another text, she said, pulling out her phone and showing him the message.

Michael's brow furrowed as he read it. They're escalating, he said, his voice grim. Whoever this is, they're trying to scare you into backing off.

Clearly, Emily said. But we're not backing off. In fact, we're here to get more answers.

Answers to what, exactly? Michael asked, crossing his arms. I've told you everything I know.

Lucas scoffed. Yeah, because cryptic warnings and half-truths are so helpful.

Michael's eyes flashed with irritation. I don't owe you an explanation.

No, but you owe one to Emily, Lucas shot back. You dragged her into this mess.

I didn't drag her into anything, Michael snapped. She was already involved— because of her father.

Emily raised her hands, stepping between them again. Okay, enough testosterone for one night. Both of you, sit down.

Reluctantly, Michael and Lucas sat on opposite ends of the couch, glaring at each other like rival wolves. Emily sat in the chair opposite them, feeling like a referee in a boxing match.

I need to know about SOLAR, she said, addressing Michael. What were they really doing? And why is this project so dangerous?

Michael leaned forward, his elbows resting on his knees. SOLAR wasn't just funding research. They were using it. The project wasn't just theoretical—it was experimental. They were trying to manipulate time on a quantum scale.

Manipulate time? Lucas echoed, disbelief coloring his tone.

Yes, Michael said. Your fathers were working on something revolutionary, but the risks were too great. Something happened—something that scared them enough to shut it all down.

Emily's stomach churned. What kind of risks?

Michael hesitated, his gaze dropping. Time manipulation isn't just about bending the rules—it's about breaking them. They were experimenting with something called temporal resonance. It's like… sending ripples through time. If they got it wrong, those ripples could turn into waves—and those waves could destroy everything.

Lucas let out a low whistle. That sounds insane.

It is, Michael admitted. But they were closer than anyone thought. Close enough that SOLAR got involved. And when things started to go wrong, SOLAR erased everything.

Emily felt a cold knot form in her chest. So my dad… and your dad… they were trying to stop it?

Michael nodded. I think so. But SOLAR didn't care about the risks—they cared about the results.

The room fell into a heavy silence as the weight of Michael's words sank in. Emily glanced at Lucas, who was staring at Michael with a mixture of suspicion and reluctant understanding.

So, what do we do now? Emily asked finally.

Michael looked at her, his expression serious. We find out where SOLAR is operating now. If they're still active, they'll have records—something that can tell us what really happened and why they're still watching us.

And how do we do that? Lucas asked, his tone skeptical.

Michael hesitated, then said, I have a contact. Someone who used to work with SOLAR.

Lucas frowned. Used to?

They got out when things went sideways, Michael said. But they might still have connections.

Great, Lucas said, his voice dripping with sarcasm. Let's just hope they don't try to kill us too.

Emily shot him a glare. Can you not?

Lucas threw up his hands. I'm just saying, this is a lot of trust to put in someone who hasn't exactly been forthcoming.

Michael ignored him, focusing on Emily. If we do this, there's no turning back. Are you sure you want to keep going?

Emily met his gaze, her resolve hardening. I don't have a choice. My dad deserves answers. And so do we.

Michael nodded, a flicker of respect in his eyes. Then we start tomorrow.

As Emily stood to leave, her phone buzzed again. This time, the message was a single line: *You're closer than you think. But so are we.*

Eleven

Out of Sight

The text *-You're closer than you think. But so are we-.* left Emily paralyzed for a moment, her phone gripped tightly in her hand. The room felt suddenly smaller, and the weight of invisible eyes watching her pressed heavily on her chest.

What is it now? Lucas asked, catching her expression.

Emily handed him the phone without a word. He read the message, his jaw tightening. That's it. We need to stop playing defense and start finding these people.

I agree, Michael said, standing. His calm demeanor had shifted into something sharper, more focused. We've been waiting for them to make a move, but it's time we get ahead of them.

Emily looked between them, both of their expressions resolute but tense. It felt like being in the middle of a storm, with two fronts colliding—and she was the eye of it.

So, what's the plan? she asked, forcing herself to stay calm.

Michael hesitated. There's a research facility outside the city. It was one of SOLAR's satellite locations before the project was shut down. If anything was left behind, it'll be there.

And this 'contact' of yours? Lucas asked, his tone laced with skepticism.

They're meeting us there, Michael said.

Meeting us? Emily repeated. Why can't they just give us the information?

Because they don't trust anyone, Michael said simply. And with good reason.

Lucas let out a low whistle. This just keeps getting better.

The next morning, Emily found herself in Michael's car, driving out of the city toward the research facility. Lucas had begrudgingly agreed to follow in his own car, claiming he needed the space to think. Emily suspected it had more to do with not wanting to sit in the same vehicle as Michael.

The tension between the two men was palpable, but Emily was too exhausted to referee. Her mind was consumed by the text messages, the cryptic notebook, and the looming shadow of SOLAR. The further they drove, the more isolated the landscape became—city streets giving way to sprawling fields and dense forests.

How did you even find this place? Emily asked, breaking the silence.

Michael kept his eyes on the road. After my father disappeared, I started looking into every connection he had to SOLAR. This facility came up in an old requisition report. It was officially decommissioned, but I have a feeling it wasn't fully abandoned.

You mean they're still using it? Emily asked, her stomach tightening.

It's possible, Michael admitted. Or they could have just left behind something useful. Either way, we need to check it out.

Emily glanced out the window, the trees blurring past. The thought of stepping into a place tied so closely to her father—and to SOLAR—sent a chill down her spine. But she couldn't turn back now. She wouldn't.

They arrived at the facility just before noon. It was a nondescript building, its concrete exterior weathered and overgrown with vines. A tall chain-link fence surrounded the property, its gate slightly ajar.

This place screams 'bad idea,' Lucas muttered as he climbed out of his car, joining Emily and Michael by the gate.

Noted, Michael said dryly. Let's try not to attract too much attention.

Lucas rolled his eyes but followed as Michael led the way inside. The air was heavy with the scent of damp earth and rust, and the building's interior was dimly lit, the windows coated with grime.

Your contact better show, Lucas muttered. I didn't drive two hours just to explore a haunted science lab.

They'll be here, Michael said, his tone clipped.

Emily glanced around, her heart pounding. The silence was oppressive, every creak of the floorboards beneath their feet echoing ominously. She couldn't shake the feeling that they were being watched.

As they entered what appeared to be a control room, Michael's phone buzzed. He checked it and nodded. They're here.

Before Emily could ask where, a shadow appeared in the doorway. She tensed, but Michael held up a hand to stop Lucas, who was already stepping forward protectively.

The figure stepped into the room—a tall woman in her late forties, with short, silver-streaked hair and sharp green eyes. She wore a plain jacket and jeans, her posture confident but wary.

Michael, she said, her voice low. It's been a long time.

Ellen, Michael replied. Thanks for coming.

Emily's mind raced. This was the mysterious contact? She looked ordinary enough, but there was an edge to her presence, like she was ready to fight or flee at a moment's notice.

This must be the girl, Ellen said, nodding toward Emily. The photographer.

Emily bristled. My name's Emily.

Right. Emily. Ellen's gaze was piercing. You look like your father.

Emily's breath caught. You knew him?

I worked with him, Ellen said simply. And with Michael's father. They were good men. Too good for what SOLAR had in mind.

What do you mean? Emily asked, her voice shaky.

Ellen's expression hardened. They wanted to create something revolutionary. But SOLAR turned it into a weapon. When your fathers realized what was happening, they tried to stop it. That's why they became targets.

Emily exchanged a glance with Michael, her chest tightening. What kind of weapon?

Ellen hesitated, then said, A way to control time itself. To rewrite events. Imagine being able to change the outcome of a war—or erase a person from history.

That's impossible, Lucas said, his skepticism returning.

Ellen's gaze was steady. Is it? Or is that just what they want you to think?

As Ellen spoke, she reached into her bag and pulled out a small device, no larger than a smartphone. She placed it on the table in front of them.

What is that? Emily asked.

It's a prototype, Ellen said. One of the few that your father managed to destroy before SOLAR shut everything down. But it still holds traces of their research. If we can decode it, we might be able to find out where SOLAR is operating now.

Michael leaned closer, studying the device. You kept this all these years?

Ellen smirked. I'm good at staying off the radar. You'll need to be, too, if you want to survive.

Emily's phone buzzed, making her jump. She checked the screen and felt her blood run cold.

We know where you are. Leave. Now.

Emily handed the phone to Michael, her hands trembling. Before he could react, the sound of a car screeching to a halt outside echoed through the building, followed by the unmistakable slam of doors.

They're here, Ellen said grimly. We need to move. Now.

Twelve

The Universe Between Us

The heavy slam of car doors echoed through the facility, sending a ripple of panic through the group. Emily's heart raced as she locked eyes with Michael, the weight of their situation sinking in.

We're out of time, Ellen said, her voice calm but urgent. We need to move, now.

What do they want? Lucas asked, his voice rising in pitch as his eyes darted toward the door.

Us, Michael said flatly, slipping the small prototype Ellen had revealed into his pocket. And any trace of what we know.

Well, that's not comforting, Lucas muttered, glancing at Emily. Are we running or fighting?

Running, Michael said sharply, already moving toward the rear exit. They're armed. We're not.

Ellen took the lead, her movements fluid and practiced. Follow me. There's another way out.

Emily grabbed her bag and fell into step behind her, adrenaline pounding in her ears. Lucas stayed close, his hand brushing against hers as if to reassure her—or himself.

The sound of boots crunching on gravel outside grew louder as they navigated through the dimly lit halls. The facility seemed like a labyrinth, every turn identical to the last, but Ellen moved with purpose, clearly familiar with the layout.

How do you even know this place? Emily whispered, her voice barely audible.

I worked here before things went sideways, Ellen replied. I know all the exits—and all the traps.

Traps? Lucas hissed.

Relax, Ellen said dryly. They're not for us.

The group rounded a corner, and Ellen pushed open a heavy metal door that led to an overgrown courtyard. The bright light of the midday sun was blinding after the dim facility, and Emily shielded her eyes as they stepped outside.

This way, Ellen said, motioning toward a gap in the chain-link fence. We'll lose them in the woods.

Emily glanced over her shoulder, dread tightening her chest as she saw figures in black tactical gear entering the building behind them. Their faces were obscured by helmets, but the glint of their weapons was unmistakable.

They're coming! she shouted, breaking into a run.

The forest was dense, the underbrush clawing at Emily's legs as she followed Ellen. Lucas stayed close behind her, his breathing labored but determined. Michael brought up the rear, glancing back occasionally to check for pursuers.

Where does this lead? Emily asked, her voice breathless.

There's an old service road about a mile from here, Ellen said. If we can reach it, we'll have a chance.

A chance at what? Lucas asked.

Not dying, Ellen said bluntly.

The sound of snapping twigs behind them sent a jolt of fear through Emily. She didn't dare look back, focusing instead on the rhythm of her feet pounding against the forest floor.

After what felt like an eternity, the group emerged onto a dirt road. Ellen paused, scanning the area with sharp eyes before motioning for them to move.

Where's this road go? Michael asked, his voice low.

There's an abandoned ranger station a few miles down, Ellen said. We can regroup there.

Emily doubled over, her hands on her knees as she tried to catch her breath. Are we even sure they're still following us?

As if in answer, a distant shout echoed through the trees, followed by the crack of gunfire.

Does that answer your question? Lucas snapped, grabbing her arm. Let's go!

They started running again, the dirt road stretching endlessly before them. Emily's lungs burned, and her legs ached, but fear kept her moving. She didn't know who these people were, but their determination to catch them was clear—and terrifying.

When they finally reached the ranger station, it was little more than a crumbling wooden cabin surrounded by overgrown weeds. Ellen forced the door open, and the group piled inside, slamming it shut behind them.

Is this place even safe? Lucas asked, his voice thick with doubt.

It's off the grid, Ellen said, leaning against the door to catch her breath. For now, that's as safe as we're going to get.

Emily sank onto a dusty bench, her chest heaving. Who the hell were those guys?

SOLAR's cleanup crew, Ellen said grimly. They're not here to negotiate.

Michael sat across from Emily, his expression dark. They want the device— and anyone who knows about it.

Lucas gestured wildly. Okay, so what's the plan? Because running isn't exactly sustainable.

We don't just run, Michael said. We go on the offensive.

Ellen raised an eyebrow. And how exactly do you plan to do that?

Michael's jaw tightened. We decode the prototype. Whatever's on it is the key to all of this. If we can figure out what SOLAR was working on, we can expose them.

And probably get killed in the process, Lucas muttered.

It's the only way to stop them, Michael said firmly. As long as they control the narrative, we're all just targets.

Emily's gaze shifted to the prototype in Michael's pocket. It looked so small, so insignificant, yet it was the reason her father had risked everything—and possibly lost his life.

We need to finish what they started, she said softly.

Michael met her eyes, his expression softening. Are you sure about this?

Emily nodded, her resolve hardening. I don't want to spend the rest of my life running.

The group set to work, Ellen taking the lead in examining the prototype. She connected it to a small laptop she'd brought, her fingers flying over the keyboard as lines of code scrolled across the screen.

This thing's heavily encrypted, she muttered. But if I can crack it…

Do you know how much time we have? Lucas asked, pacing the small room.

No, Ellen said without looking up. But I'd guess not much.

Michael stood by the window, keeping watch. Emily joined him, her nerves frayed as she peered out at the forest.

Do you really think this will work? she asked quietly.

Michael hesitated, then said, I think it's our best shot.

Emily studied him, her chest tightening. He looked so calm, so focused, but she could see the tension in his jaw, the weight he was carrying. She wanted to say something, but before she could, Ellen let out a triumphant shout.

I'm in! Ellen said, her voice laced with excitement.

Everyone crowded around the laptop as lines of data filled the screen. Maps, equations, and documents scrolled by, but one file stood out: **PROJECT TIMEBREACH**.

What is that? Emily asked, pointing at the screen.

Ellen clicked on it, and a series of diagrams appeared, showing what looked like ripples in space, converging on a single point.

It's a model, Ellen said, her voice barely above a whisper. This is what they were trying to create. A breach in time.

Michael's face darkened. And it looks like they succeeded.

Before anyone could react, the sound of tires crunching on gravel echoed outside the cabin. Ellen's face went pale. They've found us.

Thirteen

Two Choices, One Heart

The sound of tires crunching on gravel sent a jolt of fear through Emily's chest. Everyone froze, the tension in the air thick and suffocating.

They're here, Ellen said, her voice sharp and calm. We need to move. Now.

Michael moved to the window, carefully pulling back the tattered curtain. Three vehicles, he said grimly. Tactical, unmarked. They're fanning out.

Lucas swore under his breath. Great. More of the Men in Black.

Stay quiet, Ellen hissed. We don't engage unless we have no other choice.

Emily clutched her bag tightly, her father's notebook pressing against her side like a lifeline. Her pulse thundered in her ears as her gaze darted between Michael, Lucas, and the door. Every instinct told her to run, but there was nowhere to go.

What do they want? Emily asked in a low voice.

Michael didn't turn from the window. The device. And probably us.

Ellen snapped the laptop shut and shoved it into her bag. We split up. They can't follow all of us at once.

Split up? Lucas's voice rose. Are you insane?

She's right, Michael said, his tone firm. If we stay together, we're sitting ducks. We'll regroup later.

And if we don't regroup? Lucas shot back.

We will, Michael said, his eyes locking with Emily's. Trust me.

Her stomach flipped at his intensity, but she nodded. What's the plan?

Ellen pointed to a back door. Emily and Lucas, take the device and head north through the woods. There's a train station about two miles out. Michael and I will lead them south.

Lucas frowned. Why do we get stuck with the device?

Because they'll expect Michael to have it, Ellen said curtly. It's the safest move.

Lucas looked like he wanted to argue, but Emily grabbed his arm. We'll figure it out, she said quickly, not wanting to waste another second. Let's go.

The woods were dense, the branches clawing at Emily's clothes as she and Lucas moved as quietly as possible. The sound of distant voices and the crunch of boots on dry leaves made her heart pound harder with every step.

This is insane, Lucas muttered, glancing over his shoulder. We should've stayed together.

They're trying to protect us, Emily whispered. If we keep moving, we'll be okay.

Lucas huffed but didn't argue further. His grip on her arm was steady, and for the first time in their long friendship, Emily felt truly grateful for his presence.

Do you even know where we're going? he asked after a while, his voice strained.

North, Emily said, glancing at the faint sunlight breaking through the canopy. The train station's not far.

Not far, Lucas repeated with a bitter laugh. That's reassuring.

They pressed on in silence, their breath visible in the cool air. Emily's mind raced, the weight of the device in her bag a constant reminder of what was at stake. If SOLAR caught them, it wouldn't just be the end of their escape—it might be the end of everything.

Meanwhile, Michael and Ellen sprinted south, their movements precise and coordinated. Michael's mind churned as he glanced back at the cabin, hoping Emily and Lucas had gotten away. He hated leaving her, but he knew it was the only way to give them a chance.

You think they'll be okay? he asked Ellen as they pushed deeper into the woods.

If they stick to the plan, yes, Ellen said, her tone clipped. But we need to focus on losing these guys. They're professionals.

Michael nodded, his jaw tightening. He'd faced pressure before—presenting research to skeptical panels, enduring late nights in observatories—but this was different. This was survival.

Ellen suddenly stopped, holding up a hand. Wait.

Michael froze, listening intently. The forest was eerily quiet. Too quiet.

They're close, Ellen whispered, her eyes scanning the trees. We need to move faster.

Before Michael could respond, a sharp crack rang out—a gunshot.

Go! Ellen shouted, pushing him forward.

Back in the woods, Emily and Lucas stumbled onto an old dirt road. Emily's legs burned from running, but the sight of the open path gave her a brief surge of hope.

This has to lead to the train station, she said, panting.

Lucas nodded, his face pale but determined. Let's keep moving.

They hadn't gone far when the sound of a car engine roared behind them. Emily turned, her blood running cold as she saw a black SUV barreling down the road.

Run! Lucas yelled, grabbing her hand and pulling her toward the trees.

The vehicle screeched to a halt, and men in tactical gear jumped out, their shouts cutting through the air. Emily didn't look back, her heart pounding as she sprinted through the underbrush.

A branch snagged her bag, and she stumbled, nearly falling. Lucas grabbed her arm, steadying her.

Keep going! he urged.

They ran until the voices grew faint, their breaths ragged as they leaned against a tree to catch their breath.

They're not going to stop, Lucas said, his voice laced with frustration. We can't outrun them forever.

Emily pulled out the device, staring at it as if it might hold the answer. What if we use it?

Lucas gawked at her. Use it? Are you insane? We don't even know what it does!

It's the only thing they want, Emily said desperately. If we can figure out how to activate it, maybe we can—

Her words were cut off as another gunshot rang out, startling a flock of birds from the treetops.

We don't have time for this! Lucas snapped, pulling her forward. Come on!

Back on the southern side of the woods, Michael and Ellen had found temporary cover in an old hunting blind. Ellen was examining a map while Michael watched the treeline, his mind constantly drifting to Emily.

You're distracted, Ellen said without looking up.

Michael didn't deny it. They shouldn't have the device.

They're safer with it than we are, Ellen replied. You know that.

Michael exhaled, his frustration evident. I just… I need to know she's okay.

Ellen smirked faintly. You're in deep, aren't you?

Michael shot her a look. Now's not the time.

Fair enough, Ellen said, folding the map. But you'd better make it through this if you want to see her again.

In the northern woods, Emily and Lucas burst onto the edge of the train station's clearing, relief washing over them—until they saw the SUV waiting there, its engine idling, and a group of armed men standing by the platform.

Lucas grabbed Emily's arm. Now what?

Emily's gaze darted to the device in her hand, her pulse racing. We use it.

Fourteen

Falling Into Orbit

Lucas stared at Emily like she'd lost her mind. We use it? Emily, what if this thing blows up? Or creates a black hole? Or, I don't know, erases us from time?

Do you have a better idea? Emily shot back, clutching the device tightly. Her hands trembled, but she refused to let fear paralyze her. The SUV idled ominously, its occupants watching them from the shadows. We're out of options, Lucas.

Fine, Lucas muttered, running a hand through his hair. What's the plan, genius? Press a button and hope for the best?

Emily examined the device, her father's notebook open on her lap. The prototype was small and unassuming, with a sleek, metallic surface and no obvious interface—just a faintly glowing ring at its center. She flipped through the notebook, her father's hurried handwriting blurring in her vision as adrenaline coursed through her.

'Resonance point triggers convergence,' she read aloud, her voice shaky. It sounds like the device needs to be in a specific place to activate.

What place? Lucas hissed, throwing a glance over his shoulder. The men near the SUV were moving now, spreading out toward them.

Emily looked around, her mind racing. The train station platform stretched out before them, its rusted tracks cutting through the trees like veins. A faint memory surfaced—her father's voice, explaining constellations to her as a child. The stars align in patterns. Everything has a rhythm, a place where it fits perfectly.

The tracks, Emily said suddenly, her eyes widening. The tracks might be the convergence point.

Lucas blinked. You're guessing. Please tell me you're guessing.

Do you trust me or not? she shot back.

Lucas hesitated, then sighed. I'm probably going to regret this. Let's do it.

The two of them sprinted toward the tracks, ducking low to avoid being seen. The platform loomed ahead, weathered and abandoned, but it radiated an eerie sense of importance, as if the space had been waiting for this moment.

Emily dropped to her knees at the edge of the tracks, placing the device carefully between the rails. Its faint glow pulsed brighter as it made contact with the metal, and a low hum filled the air.

It's doing something, Emily whispered, her heart racing.

Yeah, great, Lucas said, his eyes darting toward the men now closing in on them. Now let's hope it's something that doesn't get us killed.

Back in the southern woods, Michael and Ellen were still evading SOLAR's cleanup crew. They had managed to throw their pursuers off their trail, but Michael's mind was elsewhere.

Emily has the device, he said, his tone edged with frustration. We need to get to her.

We can't help her if we get caught, Ellen reminded him. She's smart, Michael. She'll figure it out.

Michael shook his head, his jaw tightening. You don't know that. She's—

She's what? Fragile? Helpless? Ellen shot him a pointed look. She's more capable than you give her credit for.

Michael didn't respond, but the fear in his eyes was unmistakable. He couldn't lose her—not now.

At the tracks, the situation was spiraling. The device's hum grew louder, the air around it shimmering faintly as if bending to an invisible force. Emily flipped through the notebook again, searching for anything that might tell her what to expect.

Emily, they're coming! Lucas yelled, grabbing her arm. We have to move!

The men from the SUV were on the platform now, their weapons drawn. One of them stepped forward, his voice cold and commanding. Step away from the device.

Yeah, I don't think so, Emily said, her voice steadier than she felt.

You don't understand what you're dealing with, the man said. That prototype is unstable. If it activates here, you could destroy everything.

Funny, Emily said. That's the same thing you said about my dad, isn't it?

The man's expression didn't waver, but Emily caught the flicker of recognition in his eyes. He knew who she was—and he didn't care.

Last warning, he said. Step away.

Emily, we have to go, Lucas urged, tugging her arm.

But before Emily could move, the device let out a sharp, resonant tone that seemed to vibrate through the ground itself. The men froze, their weapons wavering, as the shimmering air around the device intensified.

It's happening, Emily whispered, a mix of awe and terror in her voice.

The air rippled, bending light and sound as the device emitted another pulse. The men shouted in confusion, some stumbling backward as the ground beneath the tracks began to vibrate.

What did you do? Lucas yelled, grabbing Emily's shoulders.

I didn't do anything! she shouted back, clutching the notebook tightly. Her father's words seemed to echo in her mind: The stars align in patterns. Everything has a rhythm.

Emily! a voice called out, cutting through the chaos. She turned to see Michael sprinting toward them, Ellen close behind.

Michael! Relief flooded her, but it was quickly replaced by panic. What's happening?

The device is reaching critical resonance, Michael said, skidding to a stop beside her. We have to stabilize it, or—

Or what? Lucas demanded.

Or it creates a breach, Michael said grimly.

Emily's heart sank. A breach in what?

Time, Michael said simply.

The men from SOLAR regrouped, their leader barking orders. Take the device—now!

One of them lunged forward, but Ellen was faster. She drew a small pistol from her jacket and fired a warning shot into the air, stopping the man in his tracks.

We don't have much time, Michael said, kneeling beside the device. Emily, give me the notebook.

She handed it to him without hesitation, her hands trembling as she watched him flip through the pages with practiced precision.

There's a way to stabilize it, he muttered, scanning the text. Your father wrote it down. We just need to—

Another pulse from the device cut him off, this one louder and more intense. The air around them seemed to fracture, shimmering like broken glass. Time itself felt off-kilter, as if the world was teetering on the edge of something monumental.

Michael! Emily shouted, her voice barely audible over the hum. Can you stop it?

Michael looked up, his expression determined. Not stop it. Control it.

Before Michael could act, the device emitted a final pulse, and the world around them seemed to ripple and collapse. In an instant, Emily felt herself pulled into a vortex of light and sound, her vision blurring as reality shifted.

When the chaos settled, she found herself standing alone—Michael, Lucas, and the men from SOLAR nowhere in sight. The tracks, the forest, the platform—they were gone.

And so were the stars.

Fifteen

A Kiss Under the Stars

Emily stumbled forward, her breath caught in her throat. The world around her was eerily quiet, the absence of sound unsettling. She stood in a place that was both familiar and alien—a field that seemed to stretch infinitely, bathed in a strange, ethereal glow. The stars, which had always been her comfort, were gone, replaced by an endless expanse of swirling light, as if she were trapped inside the cosmos itself.

Michael? she called out, her voice trembling. Lucas?

Her words were swallowed by the vast emptiness, echoing faintly before dissolving into the silence. Her heart pounded as panic began to creep in. Where was she? What had the device done?

The prototype. She glanced down at her hands, but they were empty. The device was gone, leaving her with nothing but her father's notebook and a sinking feeling of dread.

Emily! a voice rang out, distant but unmistakable.

Her heart leapt as she turned, searching the endless expanse. Michael?

I'm here! His voice grew louder, closer.

Finally, she saw him—his figure materializing through the glowing haze like a ghost returning to the living. Relief flooded her chest, and she ran toward him without hesitation, throwing her arms around him as soon as they met.

You're here, she whispered, her voice shaky with emotion. I thought—

I know, Michael said, his arms tightening around her. I thought I lost you too.

For a moment, they stood there, clinging to each other in the middle of the strange, infinite field. Emily could feel the rapid beat of his heart against hers, matching her own. It was the only real thing in this surreal place, and she held onto it like a lifeline.

What happened? she asked, pulling back just enough to meet his eyes. Where are we?

Michael's brow furrowed as he looked around, his scientist's mind clearly working overtime. The device must have activated fully. This… He gestured to the glowing expanse. This is the breach. A space between times.

Between times? Emily repeated, her voice rising with panic. You mean we're stuck?

Not necessarily, Michael said quickly, his tone soothing. The breach is like a bridge. It connects two points. We just need to figure out which ones—and how to get back to the right one.

Emily swallowed hard, her grip on his arm tightening. What if we can't?

Michael hesitated, his gaze softening. We will. I promise.

As they began to explore the strange, glowing expanse, Emily couldn't help but feel a sense of awe mixed with fear. The world around them shifted subtly with every step, the light bending and swirling as if alive. It was beautiful in a way that felt impossible to capture, even with her camera.

How do you know so much about this? she asked, glancing at Michael.

My father talked about it, Michael said, his voice quieter now. He and your dad theorized that breaches like this could exist—pockets of time and space created by resonance. They thought they could use them to study the past, maybe even the future.

Emily frowned. But why would SOLAR want that? Why is it worth all of this?

Michael's expression darkened. Because if you can control time, you can control everything. Wars, politics, people. It's not just science to them—it's power.

Emily shivered, the weight of his words sinking in. Her father had been trying to stop something far bigger than she'd ever imagined. And now, it was up to her and Michael to finish what he started.

As they walked, the air around them began to shift. The swirling light grew dimmer, and Emily felt a strange pull, like the breach itself was guiding them. The sensation made her uneasy, but Michael seemed to sense it too.

Do you feel that? he asked, his voice low.

Emily nodded. It's like… we're being drawn somewhere.

Michael stopped, his hand brushing hers. Stay close. If the breach is unstable, we could get separated.

The thought sent a chill down her spine, and she grabbed his hand without hesitation. His fingers were warm and steady, grounding her in a way that made her chest ache with emotions she couldn't name.

Michael, she said softly, glancing at him. Thank you—for staying.

He turned to her, his blue eyes meeting hers with an intensity that made her heart skip a beat. I wouldn't be anywhere else, he said, his voice low and sincere.

For a moment, the world around them seemed to pause. Emily's breath hitched as Michael stepped closer, his hand still holding hers. The light of the breach cast a soft glow on his face, making him look both impossibly real and otherworldly.

I thought I lost you, he murmured, his voice breaking slightly. And I don't think I can do this without you.

Emily's chest tightened, her emotions threatening to overwhelm her. She reached up, her fingers brushing his cheek. You're not losing me. Not now, not ever.

And then he kissed her.

It was slow, deliberate—like a promise. The warmth of his lips chased away the cold knot of fear that had settled in her chest, replacing it with something brighter, stronger. The world around them seemed to hum with energy, the swirling light reflecting the emotions surging between them.

When they finally pulled apart, Emily felt like she could breathe again, like the weight of the breach had lifted just enough for hope to creep in.

Whatever happens next, Michael said, his forehead resting against hers, we face it together.

Emily nodded, a small smile breaking through the fear. Together.

Before they could say more, the swirling light around them shifted violently, the ground beneath their feet trembling. Michael pulled Emily close, his gaze snapping to the horizon where a dark void seemed to be forming.

The breach is collapsing, he said urgently. We have to move.

Move where? Emily shouted, panic rising.

Michael's eyes locked on hers, his determination cutting through the chaos. Trust me.

Michael grabbed Emily's hand and led her toward the void, the pull growing stronger with every step. As they reached the edge, the darkness engulfed them, and Emily felt herself falling—weightless, breathless, and terrified.

When she opened her eyes, she was standing in a familiar place. The forest. The train tracks.

But Michael was gone.

Sixteen

Heartbeats and Secrets

Emily's knees buckled as she stumbled onto the familiar dirt near the train tracks. The air was cold and sharp, the chirp of crickets piercing the silence. She gasped for breath, her head spinning as she tried to orient herself.

Michael? she called out, her voice breaking. She spun around, her heart pounding as her eyes searched the dark forest. Michael!

But there was no answer. The train tracks stretched out behind her, rusted and empty. The forest loomed ahead, quiet and still. It was as if the world had decided to move on without her, leaving her stranded in its wake.

Her hands trembled as she clutched the notebook still tucked in her bag. The faint warmth of it, a reminder of her father's presence, wasn't enough to stave off the growing fear gnawing at her.

He has to be here. He has to be.

She took a shaky step forward, her breath clouding in the cold night air. The memories of the breach flashed through her mind—the glowing light, the swirling energy, Michael's steady voice telling her to trust him. And then the void.

Now there was only emptiness.

As she stumbled along the tracks, a faint sound caught her attention—the rustling of leaves, soft but deliberate. She froze, her breath catching in her throat.

Michael? she called again, her voice barely above a whisper.

But instead of Michael, a figure emerged from the shadows. Emily's pulse quickened as she recognized the tactical gear, the glint of a weapon slung over the man's shoulder. SOLAR.

She ducked instinctively, pressing herself against the embankment beside the tracks. Her mind raced. If they had found her, then they must have found the others, too. But where were they now? And how long did she have before she was next?

The footsteps receded, and Emily exhaled shakily. She had to move, and she had to figure out where Michael was. Clutching the notebook tightly, she followed the tracks deeper into the woods, her thoughts a blur of fear and determination.

Suddenly, her phone buzzed in her pocket. She fumbled to retrieve it, her heart leaping as she saw Michael's name on the screen.

Michael! she answered, her voice urgent. Where are you? Are you okay?

There was a pause, then his voice crackled through the line, faint but steady. I'm okay. Are you?

Emily's legs gave out in relief, and she sank onto the ground. I'm fine, she said, her voice trembling. But where are you? I'm back by the train tracks.

I don't know where I am, Michael admitted. The breach spit me out somewhere else. It's dark, and I think I'm near a road, but— He stopped abruptly.

What? What is it? Emily demanded.

I think they're here, Michael whispered.

Emily's blood ran cold. SOLAR?

Yeah, Michael said, his voice tight. Stay where you are. I'll find you.

Michael, no! Emily protested. If they're following you, you'll lead them right to me.

I'm not leaving you out there alone, Michael said firmly. Just stay hidden, and I'll—

A loud noise cut through the call, followed by static. Emily's heart sank as she stared at her phone, the call disconnected.

Michael, she whispered, her fear doubling.

Emily's hands curled into fists as she fought back tears. She couldn't just sit here waiting. Michael needed her as much as she needed him. And if SOLAR was closing in on him, she couldn't let him face them alone.

She pulled the notebook out of her bag, flipping through the pages frantically. Her father's words leapt off the paper: Time fractures where it weakens. Follow the signals—they'll lead you to the strongest points of connection.

Signals. Emily looked around, the faint hum of crickets and rustling leaves her only guide. But then, as if her father's words had summoned it, she saw a faint glow in the distance. It wasn't the breach, but it pulsed rhythmically, like a beacon calling to her.

She stood, clutching the notebook tightly, and began to follow the light.

The glow led her to a clearing, where a small, dilapidated cabin stood half-hidden among the trees. The light emanated from the cracks in its wooden walls, soft and rhythmic, like the heartbeat of the forest itself.

Emily hesitated, her instincts warring with her curiosity. But the pull of the light—and the faint hope that Michael might be inside—was too strong to ignore.

She pushed the door open slowly, the creak of the hinges echoing in the quiet night. Inside, the air was warm, almost suffocating, and the light pulsed brighter with each step she took.

In the center of the room stood the device, glowing faintly on a wooden table. Emily's breath caught as she approached it, her fingers brushing the cool metal surface. The hum of energy beneath her fingertips felt alive, almost familiar.

Emily.

She spun around, her heart leaping as Michael stepped into the doorway. His face was pale, his hair disheveled, but he was alive.

You're here, she breathed, rushing to him.

Michael caught her in his arms, holding her tightly. I thought I'd lost you.

Not a chance, Emily said, her voice muffled against his chest. But SOLAR—

They're closing in, Michael said grimly. We don't have much time.

He released her and moved toward the device, his expression dark as he studied it. This must be what pulled us here. It's connected to the breach.

Can we use it? Emily asked, her voice trembling.

Michael hesitated, then nodded. If we can synchronize it, we might be able to reopen the breach—and use it to get out of here.

Emily glanced at the notebook, her father's notes running through her mind. He wrote about synchronization—about finding the strongest point of connection. Could this be it?

It has to be, Michael said. But activating it will take time. We need to hold them off long enough to finish.

Emily swallowed hard, the weight of the situation crashing over her. Then let's do it.

As Michael began working on the device, the sound of boots crunching on leaves reached Emily's ears. She turned toward the door, her heart racing as the first shadow appeared outside.

We're out of time, Michael said, his voice steady despite the fear in his eyes. Get ready.

Seventeen

The Edge of the Breach

The first shadow outside the cabin moved with deliberate precision. Emily's pulse quickened as she caught sight of a figure in tactical gear, their silhouette blending with the darkness. They weren't in the middle of nowhere anymore—they were surrounded.

Michael, she whispered, her voice trembling. They're here.

I know, he said quietly, his hands steady as he adjusted the settings on the device. I need more time.

Emily's grip on her father's notebook tightened. How much more time?

Michael glanced at her, the faint glow of the device illuminating his face. Five minutes, maybe less.

We don't have five minutes, she said, her panic rising.

Michael met her gaze, his blue eyes calm and resolute. We'll make it work.

Before she could respond, the first man appeared in the doorway, his weapon drawn. He froze when he saw them, his gaze locking on the device.

Step away, he ordered, his voice sharp.

Emily's heart raced as she moved instinctively in front of the device. No.

The man hesitated, clearly not expecting resistance. His weapon shifted slightly, the barrel now pointed directly at her.

Emily, Michael said under his breath, his tone a warning.

I'm not letting them take it, she said firmly, her fear overridden by determination. They're not winning this.

The man took a step forward, but before he could say anything, a loud crack echoed through the cabin. He flinched, glancing over his shoulder as a second man shouted from outside.

Emily and Michael exchanged a look of confusion—then realization. Someone else was out there.

Outside the cabin, chaos erupted. Gunfire rang out, sharp and precise, cutting through the stillness of the forest. Shouts followed, the unmistakable sound of orders being barked. The SOLAR operatives scrambled, their focus split between the unknown threat and the cabin.

Emily peered through the window, her breath catching as she saw Lucas emerge from the shadows, armed with a makeshift club. His face was pale but resolute as he swung at one of the operatives, catching him off guard.

Lucas! she shouted, her voice breaking.

Michael moved to the window, his eyes widening. Is he insane?

Apparently, Emily muttered, a strange mix of fear and admiration surging through her. We have to help him.

No, Michael said firmly, grabbing her arm. You stay here. I'll go.

Like hell you will, Emily shot back, pulling free. You need to finish with the device.

Michael hesitated, torn between logic and instinct. Finally, he nodded, his jaw tightening. Stay low. If anything happens—

Nothing's going to happen, Emily interrupted. Just keep working.

Emily slipped out the back of the cabin, the cool night air biting at her skin. The forest was alive with movement, shadows darting between the trees as the operatives regrouped. She crouched low, her heart pounding as she made her way toward Lucas.

He was pinned against a tree, his makeshift weapon clutched tightly in his hands as two operatives closed in on him. One of them raised his weapon, but before he could fire, Emily grabbed a rock and hurled it with all her strength. It hit him square in the helmet, and he stumbled, cursing loudly.

Lucas, move! she shouted.

Lucas didn't need to be told twice. He ducked under the second operative's arm and sprinted toward her, his breaths coming in ragged gasps.

What the hell are you doing here? he demanded as they crouched behind a fallen log.

Saving your ass, she shot back, peeking over the edge of the log. You're welcome, by the way.

Lucas shook his head, a faint grin breaking through his fear. You're insane, you know that?

Pot, meet kettle, Emily muttered, her eyes scanning the shadows for movement.

Back in the cabin, Michael worked furiously, his fingers flying over the controls of the device. The glow intensified, the air around it shimmering faintly as the resonance began to build.

Come on, he muttered, his focus unwavering. Almost there.

Ellen's voice echoed in his mind, a memory from years ago: If you push too far, the breach won't just open—it'll pull everything in.

Michael exhaled slowly, steadying his hands. He couldn't afford to get this wrong. Not now.

Outside, the battle continued. Emily and Lucas moved in tandem, their years of friendship translating into an unspoken understanding. They managed to evade the operatives, using the dense forest to their advantage.

But their luck ran out when they reached the edge of the clearing. Two more operatives appeared, their weapons aimed directly at them.

Stop, one of them ordered, his voice cold. Hands where we can see them.

Emily's mind raced. They were outnumbered, unarmed, and out of options. Her gaze flicked to Lucas, who looked equally panicked.

Then, without warning, the operatives were taken down by two precise shots. Emily and Lucas turned to see Ellen stepping out of the shadows, her pistol still raised.

You're welcome, she said, her tone dry.

Ellen? Emily gasped, relief flooding her chest. How did you—?

No time, Ellen interrupted, motioning toward the cabin. We need to move. Now.

The three of them burst back into the cabin just as the device let out a low, resonant hum. Michael looked up, his expression a mix of relief and urgency.

It's ready, he said, his voice steady. But once it activates, we only have seconds to get through the breach.

Then let's not waste them, Ellen said, positioning herself by the door. I'll hold them off.

You're not coming with us? Emily asked, her heart sinking.

Ellen gave her a small, sad smile. My fight's here. Yours is on the other side.

Before Emily could argue, Ellen fired another shot, the sound jolting them into action.

Emily, Michael said, grabbing her hand. Now

As Michael activated the device, the air around them fractured, the familiar glow of the breach consuming the room. Emily felt herself being pulled forward, her grip on Michael's hand tightening as the world dissolved into light and sound.

When the chaos settled, she opened her eyes to find herself in a bustling city street—cars honking, people walking, and skyscrapers towering above her. She turned, but Michael wasn't there.

Michael? she whispered, her voice lost in the noise of the city.

She was alone. Again.

Eighteen

Parallel Paths

Emily stood frozen in the middle of the bustling city street, her heart hammering in her chest. The roar of traffic and the chatter of passersby surrounded her, an overwhelming cacophony after the eerie stillness of the breach. Her eyes darted around, searching desperately for any sign of Michael.

But he was gone.

Michael! she shouted, her voice cracking. A few pedestrians shot her curious glances, but no one stopped. She felt a sharp pang of panic. Where am I?

She spun around, taking in her surroundings. The towering skyscrapers, the distinct yellow cabs, the rush of people glued to their phones—it was New York City. But something felt… off. The air felt heavier, the sky dimmer, as if the world had shifted slightly out of alignment.

The notebook was still clutched in her hands, its familiar weight grounding her. Focus, Emily. Think.

She moved to the edge of the sidewalk, leaning against a lamppost as she tried to calm her breathing. She couldn't fall apart now. Michael was out there somewhere, and she had to find him. But first, she needed to figure out when—and where—she was.

Emily ducked into a nearby coffee shop, the warm aroma of espresso and baked goods temporarily soothing her nerves. She slid into a corner booth and pulled out her phone, half expecting it not to work. To her surprise, it powered on, and a quick glance at the date made her stomach flip.

It wasn't today. It wasn't even yesterday. She was two weeks in the future.

Her heart raced as she stared at the screen. The breach hadn't just displaced her—it had sent her forward in time. The realization sent a chill through her. If she was two weeks ahead, where was Michael? Had he ended up in the same timeline? Or had the breach scattered them across time like debris in a storm?

Her fingers hovered over her phone, debating whether to call Lucas. If he had made it through the breach too, he might already be looking for her. Or worse, he might not have made it out at all.

She dialed his number, her hands shaking. The call rang three times before going to voicemail.

Lucas, it's me, she said, her voice trembling. I'm okay—I think—but I'm two weeks in the future. Please call me if you get this. And… if you're with Michael, tell him I'm looking for him.

She hung up, her chest tight with worry. What if no one made it through but me?

The hours ticked by as Emily tried to piece together a plan. She scoured her father's notebook, hoping for clues, but the cryptic notes only deepened her frustration. The phrase parallel resonance pathways appeared repeatedly, accompanied by diagrams of intersecting timelines and nodes. The device had created a breach, but the breach itself was unstable—like a rickety bridge that could collapse at any moment.

I need to find Michael, she thought, her determination hardening. If anyone can figure this out, it's him.

Her thoughts were interrupted by the buzz of her phone. A message popped up on the screen, and her breath caught when she saw the sender.

It was Michael.

The message was short and cryptic, but it was enough to send her bolting out of the coffee shop.

Meet me at the observatory. Midnight.

Her heart soared with relief. He was alive—and he was here. But her relief was short-lived as questions flooded her mind. How had he found her? Had he been stuck here, waiting for her this whole time? And why the observatory?

She pushed the doubts aside, focusing instead on the relief of knowing he was safe. She had a destination now, a purpose. She wasn't alone anymore.

By the time Emily arrived at the Hayden Planetarium, the city had settled into its late-night rhythm. The streets were quieter, the crowds thinner, but her nerves were sharper than ever. She stood outside the building, its familiar dome glowing faintly against the night sky.

Michael? she called softly as she stepped inside.

The echo of her footsteps followed her as she made her way to the main observatory. The room was dimly lit, the massive telescope casting long shadows across the floor. For a moment, the silence was overwhelming, and she feared she had misunderstood the message.

But then she saw him.

Michael stood near the telescope, his back to her. Relief flooded her chest, and she ran to him without hesitation.

Michael! she called, her voice breaking.

He turned just in time to catch her as she threw her arms around him. The warmth of his embrace, the steady beat of his heart against hers—it was real. He was real.

You made it, she whispered, tears streaming down her face.

Michael pulled back just enough to look at her, his blue eyes filled with both relief and guilt. I thought I lost you.

Emily shook her head. I thought I lost you. What happened? How did we get separated?

Michael hesitated, his jaw tightening. The breach is unstable. It didn't just send us through time—it scattered us. I've been here for two weeks, trying to figure out where you were.

Her chest tightened. You've been here all this time?

He nodded. I sent the message as soon as I figured out how to stabilize the breach. But it's still fragile, Emily. If we don't fix this, it could collapse completely.

She swallowed hard, the weight of his words sinking in. How do we fix it?

Michael reached into his bag and pulled out the device. It was faintly cracked, its glow dimmer than before. We need to recalibrate the resonance. If we can align the breach's pathways, we can reopen it and stabilize the timeline.

Emily's stomach twisted. And if we can't?

Michael met her gaze, his expression grim. Then the timeline fractures completely. And we might not have another chance.

As Emily reached for the device, the planetarium's lights flickered, and a deep hum filled the room. Michael froze, his eyes darting to the entrance.

They found us, he said, his voice low.

The sound of boots echoed through the observatory, followed by the unmistakable voice of a SOLAR operative. You've run far enough. Hand it over, Dr. Blake.

Nineteen

The Flight Plan

Emily's breath hitched at the sound of the SOLAR operative's voice echoing through the observatory. She instinctively stepped closer to Michael, her heart pounding. He tightened his grip on the device, his jaw clenched as his eyes scanned the room for an escape route.

We don't have time for this, Michael whispered, his voice low. They'll take the device—and us—if we let them.

Emily swallowed hard, her mind racing. What do we do?

Michael glanced at her, his expression steady despite the chaos closing in around them. We run.

Before Emily could protest, Michael grabbed her hand and pulled her toward the side exit. The sound of boots on the marble floor grew louder, the operatives closing in with military precision.

This way, Michael said, leading her down a narrow hallway that spiraled toward the back of the observatory. The air felt colder, the distant hum of the planetarium's machinery vibrating through the walls. Emily clutched her father's notebook tightly, her legs burning as they ran.

Behind them, a voice barked orders. They're heading toward the service wing. Don't let them leave the building.

Michael cursed under his breath. They're cutting us off.

Emily glanced back, her heart leaping as she saw shadows moving quickly through the dimly lit hallway. We're not going to make it, Michael.

Yes, we are, he said firmly, his hand tightening around hers.

They burst through a heavy door into the planetarium's storage wing, where rows of equipment and crates were stacked haphazardly. Michael led her toward a small loading dock, its garage-style door partially open to the cool night air.

This is it, Michael said, pulling the device from his bag. We have to recalibrate it now.

Emily stared at him, her chest heaving. Are you serious? They're right behind us.

Michael met her gaze, his blue eyes unwavering. If we don't do this, they'll keep chasing us forever. We have to stabilize the breach here and now.

Emily hesitated, her instincts screaming at her to keep running. But Michael's conviction, the sheer determination in his voice, anchored her. She nodded. Tell me what to do.

Michael knelt by the device, placing it on the concrete floor of the loading dock. Its faint glow pulsed erratically, the hum growing louder as he adjusted the settings. Emily crouched beside him, flipping through her father's notebook for anything that might help.

Here, she said, pointing to a diagram labeled Resonance Stability Protocol. It says you need to align the temporal nodes manually.

Michael frowned. That's risky. If I get the alignment wrong—

We don't have a choice, Emily said firmly. You can do this, Michael.

His jaw tightened as he nodded, his hands moving quickly over the device. The glow brightened, casting eerie shadows across the walls. Emily held her breath, the tension in the air thick enough to cut.

Suddenly, the door behind them slammed open, and three SOLAR operatives stormed in, their weapons raised.

Don't move! one of them barked.

Emily's heart raced as she instinctively stepped in front of the device, shielding Michael with her body. Stay back! she shouted, her voice shaking but defiant.

The lead operative took a step forward, his weapon trained on her. You don't understand what you're dealing with. That device is unstable. If you activate it, you'll tear a hole in the timeline.

Michael rose slowly, his hands raised to show he wasn't a threat. You're lying, he said, his voice steady. You don't want to stabilize the timeline—you want to control it.

The operative's expression didn't waver. Give us the device, Dr. Blake. This is your last warning.

Emily's mind raced. She glanced at Michael, whose gaze flicked to the notebook in her hands. He gave her the faintest nod—a silent signal.

Without thinking, Emily hurled the notebook toward the operatives. It wasn't much of a distraction, but it was enough. Michael lunged for the device, his hands flying over the controls as he initiated the alignment.

The operatives shouted, their weapons trained on him, but Emily moved instinctively, grabbing the nearest crate and shoving it toward them. It crashed into their legs, sending them stumbling backward.

Emily, get down! Michael shouted.

She dropped to the ground just as the device emitted a blinding flash of light. The air around them seemed to ripple and twist, the hum growing into a deafening roar. Emily covered her head, her ears ringing as the room seemed to fold in on itself.

When the light faded, Emily opened her eyes to find the operatives sprawled on the ground, disoriented. Michael was kneeling by the device, his face pale but triumphant.

It's done, he said, his voice shaky. The breach is stable—for now.

Emily crawled to his side, her hands trembling. What does that mean? Did we fix it?

Michael hesitated, his gaze shifting to the glowing device. We stopped the collapse, but it's not over. We need to reset the resonance point at its origin—the observatory where it all began.

Her stomach sank. You mean the Hayden Planetarium?

Michael shook his head. No. The original observatory. The one where our fathers worked.

Emily's breath caught. That place has been shut down for decades.

I know, Michael said quietly. But it's the only way.

Before Emily could respond, the sound of sirens filled the air. The SOLAR operatives, now regaining their composure, scrambled to their feet.

We need to go, Michael said, grabbing the device. He pulled Emily to her feet, and they sprinted toward the open loading dock.

As they ran into the night, Emily's mind raced. The thought of returning to her father's old observatory, the place where everything had started, filled her with equal parts fear and determination. This wasn't just about fixing the breach anymore—it was about uncovering the truth.

As they disappeared into the darkness, Emily's phone buzzed in her pocket. She pulled it out and froze when she saw the message.

The observatory is waiting. Come alone, or you'll lose everything.

Twenty

A Leap of Faith

The cryptic message glowed on Emily's phone screen: *The observatory is waiting. Come alone, or you'll lose everything.*

Her breath caught in her throat, and the weight of the words sank in like a stone. Who had sent it? And how could they possibly know what she and Michael were planning? Her stomach twisted as the implications hit her. Come alone.

Michael glanced at her as they ran through the deserted streets. What's wrong?

Emily hesitated, clutching the phone tightly. It's another message, she said finally, her voice low.

Michael stopped, turning to face her. His expression hardened as he read the text over her shoulder. No, he said immediately. You're not going alone.

They might know something, Emily said, her voice trembling. This could be a trap, but it could also be a way to end this.

Michael's jaw tightened. That's exactly why you're not going. If they know about the observatory, they know about the breach. They're playing you.

But what if they're not? Emily shot back, her frustration bubbling over. What if this is the only way to get answers?

Michael took a step closer, his voice low but intense. Emily, I know you're scared. I am too. But if you go in there alone, you're giving them exactly what they want. We're stronger together.

His words hung in the air, a quiet plea that tugged at her resolve. Emily's chest tightened. She didn't want to leave Michael behind, not after everything they'd been through. But the message felt personal, like whoever had sent it knew exactly how to get under her skin.

We don't have time to argue, she said finally. We're going to the observatory, together. But if I think this is the only way to stop them, you have to trust me.

Michael stared at her, his expression torn. Finally, he nodded. Okay. Together.

The observatory loomed on the horizon, its skeletal structure silhouetted against the pale light of the rising moon. The air felt heavier here, charged with a strange energy that made the hairs on the back of Emily's neck stand up. This was the place where everything had started—the experiments, the breach, the secrets her father had died protecting.

It looks abandoned, Michael said, his voice barely above a whisper.

Emily nodded, clutching her bag tightly. It's been shut down for years.

Which makes it the perfect place for SOLAR to operate in secret, Michael muttered.

The front gates were rusted and twisted, hanging open like a broken jaw. They slipped through the opening, moving cautiously toward the main building. Shadows danced across the cracked pavement, the only sound the crunch of their footsteps.

Emily's phone buzzed again, and she flinched. Michael glanced at her, his expression wary as she checked the screen.

Inside. Top floor.

Her heart sank. Whoever was sending these messages wasn't just watching—they were leading her.

The interior of the observatory was dark and oppressive, the air thick with dust and decay. Emily's flashlight cut through the gloom, illuminating shattered equipment, broken glass, and faded diagrams pinned to the walls. The remnants of her father's work.

Michael moved beside her, his own flashlight sweeping across the room. This is where it happened, he said quietly, his voice tinged with awe and sadness.

Emily swallowed hard, the weight of the past pressing down on her. He was trying to stop it, she murmured. Whatever SOLAR wanted to do with the breach… he knew it was too dangerous.

Michael nodded, his jaw tightening. And now it's up to us.

The climb to the top floor was grueling, the creaking stairs threatening to give way beneath their weight. When they finally reached the observation deck, Emily's breath caught. The massive telescope stood in the center of the room, its once-gleaming surface tarnished with age. But the space wasn't abandoned.

A man stood near the telescope, his back to them. He was tall and broad-shouldered, dressed in a dark suit that seemed out of place in the dilapidated observatory. The air around him felt charged, as if the breach itself had followed him here.

Welcome, Emily, he said, his voice calm and measured. He turned slowly, revealing a face that sent a jolt of recognition through her.

Her hands trembled. You… you worked with my father.

The man smiled faintly. Dr. Carter was a brilliant man. A visionary, like your friend Michael here.

Michael stiffened, stepping protectively in front of Emily. Who are you?

My name isn't important, the man said, his gaze shifting to the device in Michael's hands. What matters is that you've brought exactly what we need to finish what your fathers started.

Emily's mind raced. What are you talking about? My father wanted to stop this.

Because he didn't understand its potential, the man said, his tone sharp. The breach isn't a threat—it's an opportunity. Imagine controlling time itself, rewriting history to correct its mistakes.

Michael's eyes narrowed. And by 'correct,' you mean control.

The man shrugged. Call it what you will. But the power is here, and it's time to harness it.

Emily shook her head, her voice trembling with anger. You're insane. My father died trying to stop you.

And his death won't be in vain, the man said, his voice softening. But I need your help, Emily. The breach is fragile, and only you can stabilize it. Your father's work—his legacy—is the key.

No, Michael said firmly, stepping closer. We're not helping you.

The man's expression hardened. You don't have a choice.

The lights in the observatory flickered, and the air around them shimmered with an eerie glow. The breach was opening again, its energy crackling through the room.

The man smiled, his eyes gleaming. It's already begun.

Twenty-One

Between Two Worlds

The crackling energy of the breach consumed the room, the air vibrating with an intensity that made Emily's bones ache. The glow around the telescope pulsed like a heartbeat, brightening with each second. Emily clutched her father's notebook tightly, her knuckles white.

Emily, don't listen to him, Michael said sharply, stepping closer to her. This isn't about fixing the past—it's about controlling it. That's all they've ever wanted.

The man standing by the telescope smiled faintly, his confidence unshaken. Your father had the same reservations, Emily. But he saw the truth in the end. The breach isn't destruction—it's salvation.

You don't know that, Emily shot back, her voice shaking. He wanted to stop this because it was too dangerous.

The man took a step toward her, his gaze softening. He wanted to protect you. But the work was never about stopping time—it was about saving it. The device you hold, the resonance point, the notebook—it all leads here.

You're the only one who can finish it.

Michael moved protectively in front of Emily, his voice low and furious. If this breach collapses, you'll destroy everything.

Not if we control it, the man said calmly, his eyes fixed on Emily. And that's why we need her.

The lights flickered again, and the glow of the breach intensified, illuminating the entire observatory in a surreal, otherworldly light. Emily's heart pounded as she watched the shimmering energy ripple through the air, distorting reality itself.

Michael leaned closer to her, his voice urgent. Emily, we have to stop this. The longer the breach stays open, the more unstable it becomes. It could collapse and take everything with it.

Emily stared at the device in her hands, its faint hum growing louder as the breach's energy resonated with it. Her father's notes swirled in her mind, fragments of equations and warnings that now seemed more important than ever.

The breach connects two points, she murmured, her voice barely audible. If we stabilize it, we can close it without collapsing everything.

Michael's brow furrowed. Stabilize it how?

She flipped through the notebook, her fingers trembling. Her father's notes had hinted at a way to control the breach's resonance, aligning the temporal pathways to create balance. But the process was dangerous, and one wrong move could trigger a collapse.

You have no idea what you're doing, the man said, his tone sharp now. The breach isn't meant to be closed—it's meant to be used.

Emily's head snapped up, her anger flaring. Used for what? So you can rewrite history to suit yourself?

The man's smile returned, cold and calculated. To rewrite mistakes. To reshape the future.

Michael stepped forward, his voice cutting through the tension. You don't want to fix the timeline—you want to control it. That's why SOLAR buried this project. Even they knew it was too dangerous.

The man's expression darkened. SOLAR was afraid of progress. But you, Emily—you can see the truth. Your father would have wanted you to finish what he started.

Emily's breath caught at the mention of her father. Doubt crept in, tangling with the fear and determination already weighing on her. What if the man was right? What if her father's work had been more than just a warning?

Emily, Michael said softly, his hand brushing her arm. She turned to him, her chest tightening at the intensity in his gaze. Your father trusted you to protect this, not to let them twist it into something dangerous. You know what's right.

She nodded slowly, her resolve hardening. We stabilize it. We close the breach.

The man's face twisted with frustration. You're making a mistake. If you close the breach, you'll lose everything. The answers you're looking for—they're in there.

Emily met his gaze, her voice steady. Some questions aren't meant to be answered.

As the breach's energy grew more erratic, Emily knelt by the device, flipping through her father's notes for the stabilization sequence. Michael crouched beside her, his hands steady as he adjusted the settings.

Tell me what to do, Michael said.

Emily nodded, pointing to a diagram in the notebook. We need to synchronize the resonance points with the breach's energy. If we get the timing right, it'll stabilize long enough to close it.

And if we get it wrong? Michael asked, his voice grim.

Emily swallowed hard. Then it collapses. Everything collapses.

Michael's hand briefly brushed hers, a silent promise. We won't get it wrong.

The man moved toward them, his voice rising. If you do this, you'll destroy everything your father worked for!

Emily ignored him, her focus laser-sharp as she adjusted the device. The hum grew louder, the air around them shimmering as the breach's energy began to synchronize.

Almost there, she whispered.

But the man wasn't done. He lunged toward them, his hand reaching for the device. Michael reacted instantly, shoving him backward. They grappled briefly, the man's strength surprising as he tried to push past Michael.

Emily, hurry! Michael shouted.

The breach pulsed violently, the energy surging as if it were fighting back. Emily's hands shook as she entered the final sequence, the device vibrating in her grip. The hum reached a deafening pitch, and the entire room seemed to tilt as the breach's glow brightened.

With a final, desperate push, Emily activated the stabilization protocol. The device emitted a sharp tone, and the energy around the breach began to shift. The chaotic ripples smoothed into steady waves, the light dimming as the breach stabilized.

It's working! she shouted.

But the man wasn't finished. With a furious roar, he broke free from Michael and lunged for the device. Emily screamed as his hand connected, the sudden surge of energy sending a shockwave through the room.

The breach pulsed violently, the stabilization faltering as the man's interference disrupted the sequence. The device sparked, its glow flickering erratically.

And then, with a deafening roar, the breach exploded outward, engulfing everything in a blinding light.

When Emily opened her eyes, she was somewhere else entirely. The observatory was gone.

And she was alone. Again.

Twenty-Two

The Fractured Moment

Emily stumbled as the blinding light faded, her surroundings coming into focus. She found herself in an unfamiliar place—a quiet meadow bathed in golden light. The air was warm, and the faint scent of wildflowers lingered. It was beautiful but unsettling, like a dream she couldn't wake from.

Michael? she called out, her voice trembling.

The only response was the rustling of leaves in the gentle breeze. Her chest tightened as panic set in. The device was gone. The notebook was gone. And Michael was gone.

No, she whispered, her hands clutching at the fabric of her jacket. No, no, no.

She spun around, searching desperately for any sign of him, or of the observatory, or the breach. But there was nothing—just the endless meadow and an overwhelming sense of isolation.

Emily sank to her knees, tears pricking her eyes. She had no idea where—or when—she was. The last thing she remembered was the breach stabilizing, the man's interference, and the surge of energy that had consumed everything. Now, she was trapped in a place that felt disconnected from reality, a fragment of time that didn't belong.

Her fingers curled into fists, the grass cool beneath her palms. I can't stay here. Michael needs me. I have to get back.

She stood shakily, forcing herself to think. If the breach had brought her here, there had to be a way to use it to return. Her father's notes had hinted at the idea of temporal anchors—places or moments tied to the resonance of the breach. Maybe this meadow was one of them.

Her gaze swept the horizon, looking for anything unusual. And then she saw it: a faint shimmer in the distance, like heat rising from asphalt. It pulsed faintly, the rhythm oddly familiar.

The breach.

Emily walked cautiously toward the shimmer, her heart pounding with every step. As she drew closer, the air grew warmer, the energy around her vibrating softly. The shimmer resolved into a crackling distortion in the air—a tear, small but unmistakable. The breach wasn't fully closed—it was trying to stabilize.

This is it, she murmured, a flicker of hope breaking through her fear.

But as she reached for the breach, a voice stopped her.

Emily.

She froze, her hand hovering just inches from the tear. Slowly, she turned, her breath catching in her throat.

Standing a few feet away was her father.

Dad? she whispered, her voice breaking. The sight of him, alive and whole, made her knees weak. His familiar, kind eyes, his slightly crooked smile—it was all real. Too real.

It's me, sweetheart, he said softly, taking a cautious step forward.

Tears spilled down her cheeks as she stumbled toward him, her heart aching with relief and confusion. But... how? You're—

Gone, he finished gently. I know. But time doesn't work the way we think it does. Not here.

She shook her head, struggling to make sense of his words. Am I dead? Is this... the afterlife?

No, he said quickly, his voice firm. You're caught in a temporal echo—a fragment of the breach. It brought us together, but it won't last.

Her hands trembled as she reached for him, afraid he might disappear if she touched him. But when her fingers brushed his, he felt solid, real. I don't understand. What do I do?

You have to go back, he said, his tone urgent now. The breach is unstable, and if you don't close it properly, it'll collapse completely. Everything we tried to protect will be lost.

Emily's chest tightened. But how? The device—it's gone.

Her father placed his hands on her shoulders, his touch grounding her. The device was just a tool. The real key is you.

Me? she whispered, her voice cracking.

The resonance, he explained. It's tied to you, to your connection to time itself. You've been at the center of this all along.

Tears blurred her vision as she shook her head. But I don't know how to fix it.

You do, he said, his voice steady and filled with quiet conviction. You've always known. Trust yourself.

The shimmer behind her pulsed brighter, its rhythm accelerating. Emily glanced over her shoulder, the tear in the air growing wider, its edges crackling with energy.

It's time, her father said, his voice softening. You can do this.

Her throat tightened as she looked back at him. Will I see you again?

He smiled sadly. Not like this. But I'm always with you, Emily. Always.

Her chest ached as she stepped back, her eyes locked on his. I love you, Dad.

I love you too, he said, his voice breaking slightly. Now go.

Emily turned toward the breach, her heart pounding as the energy swirled around her. She reached out, her fingers brushing the crackling edge, and the world tilted sharply. A deafening roar filled her ears, and she felt herself being pulled forward, weightless and breathless.

The meadow dissolved into light and sound, and for a moment, there was nothing but the sensation of falling.

When Emily opened her eyes, she was back in the observatory. The air was thick with smoke, and the faint hum of the breach vibrated through the room. Michael was kneeling near the telescope, his face pale and streaked with soot. His eyes widened when he saw her.

Emily! he shouted, scrambling to his feet.

Relief flooded her chest as she ran to him, throwing her arms around his neck. He held her tightly, his breath shaky. I thought you were gone.

I'm here, she whispered, her voice thick with emotion. And I know what to do.

Emily pulled back, her gaze fierce as she turned toward the breach, now crackling violently in the center of the room. She reached for Michael's hand, her voice steady despite the chaos.

Together, she said.

Michael nodded, his grip tightening. Together.

As they stepped toward the breach, the air around them fractured, the light surging brighter than ever.

Twenty-Three

Closing the Loop

The breach glowed like a furious wound in the fabric of reality, its energy radiating in unstable waves. The observatory trembled under its power, broken glass and debris vibrating across the floor. Emily tightened her grip on Michael's hand as they approached, her heart pounding with both fear and determination.

It's going to collapse, Michael said, his voice barely audible over the deafening hum. We don't have much time.

Emily nodded, the memory of her father's words grounding her. The key is you. Trust yourself.

She turned to Michael, her gaze steady. We need to align the resonance manually. The breach is responding to me—it's connected to my energy. But I can't do it alone.

Michael studied her, his jaw tightening with resolve. Then let's finish this.

The notebook was gone, the device barely functioning, but Emily didn't need them anymore. Her father's lessons, his scribbled notes, and the countless hours she'd spent searching for answers had all led her to this moment. She knelt near the breach, the intense heat making her skin prickle, and placed her hands just inches from its edge. The energy pulsed under her palms, alive and chaotic.

Michael crouched beside her, his movements precise as he adjusted the device's settings. Sparks flew as it struggled to keep up with the breach's fluctuations, but the faint hum grew steadier under his touch.

What's next? he asked, glancing at her.

Emily closed her eyes, focusing on the rhythm of the breach. It wasn't random—it was a pattern, a pulse that resonated deep within her. She took a deep breath and let the energy guide her.

Match the pulse, she said, her voice calm despite the chaos. We need to stabilize the frequency.

Michael nodded, his fingers flying over the device's controls. The hum grew louder, syncing with the breach's erratic rhythm. Emily felt the energy shift, responding to their efforts. It was working—but it wasn't enough.

Something's wrong, Michael muttered, his brow furrowing. The alignment isn't holding.

Emily's chest tightened. The breach was fighting back, its energy surging wildly as if resisting their control. Her father's words echoed in her mind: It's tied to you. Trust yourself.

I have to go in, she said suddenly, her voice steady.

Michael froze, his head snapping toward her. What? No. Absolutely not.

The breach is connected to me, she insisted. If I stabilize it from the inside, it'll hold.

You don't even know if that's possible, Michael argued, his voice rising. You could get trapped—or worse.

Emily turned to him, her eyes filled with quiet determination. If I don't, it collapses. And we lose everything.

Michael's expression softened, fear and anger warring in his gaze. There has to be another way.

There isn't, she said gently. But I need you to trust me, Michael. Just like I trust you.

His throat worked as he swallowed hard. I can't lose you, Emily.

You won't, she said, her voice breaking. I promise.

Before he could stop her, Emily reached for the breach. The energy wrapped around her like a living thing, pulling her forward. She gasped as the world tilted, the observatory dissolving into light and sound. For a moment, she felt weightless, suspended in the heart of the breach.

The energy was overwhelming, but it wasn't chaotic—it was alive, pulsing with a rhythm that resonated deep within her. She closed her eyes, letting the connection guide her. Slowly, she reached out with her mind, aligning her energy with the breach's chaotic waves.

The resonance steadied, the wild fluctuations smoothing into a harmonious pulse. Emily felt the breach respond, its energy calming as the balance restored itself. She was part of it now—woven into its fabric, holding it together.

Outside the breach, Michael watched in awe as the chaotic energy began to stabilize. The trembling observatory grew still, the glow of the breach softening into a steady light. His heart ached with fear and admiration as he watched Emily, her figure barely visible within the swirling energy.

She's doing it, he whispered, his voice filled with awe.

But then the breach pulsed violently, and Emily cried out, her body trembling under the strain.

Emily! Michael shouted, moving closer. The breach surged, its energy flaring like a dying star.

Emily's voice echoed faintly, filled with pain and determination. It's almost done. Just a little longer.

Michael's fists clenched as he fought the urge to pull her back. He knew she was right—the breach needed her to stabilize. But the thought of losing her was unbearable.

Hold on, he said, his voice breaking. You're almost there.

The breach's light dimmed, its energy stabilizing into a smooth, steady pulse. Emily exhaled shakily, her connection to the breach solidifying. She could feel it now—a web of timelines, each thread shimmering with potential. The chaos had given way to harmony, and for the first time, she understood.

Time wasn't a line or a loop—it was a tapestry, woven from countless choices and possibilities. And she was part of it, her energy a single, vital thread.

With one final surge of will, Emily anchored the breach, sealing it with a wave of calm that rippled through the observatory. The light faded, and the room fell silent.

When Emily opened her eyes, she was back in the observatory. The breach was gone, its energy dissipated into the still night air. She collapsed onto the floor, her body trembling with exhaustion.

Emily! Michael was at her side in an instant, his arms wrapping around her. Relief flooded his voice as he pulled her close. You did it.

She nodded weakly, her head resting against his shoulder. It's over.

Michael held her tightly, his voice breaking. I thought I lost you.

You never will, she whispered, her eyes closing as exhaustion overtook her. Not as long as we're together.

Twenty-Four

Epilogue: The Time Between Stars

The observatory rooftop was silent except for the soft whisper of the wind, carrying with it a rare moment of peace. The stars above stretched endlessly, their light steady and unbroken. For the first time in what felt like forever, Emily wasn't afraid of what the future held—or what the past might demand.

She and Michael stood side by side, their fingers intertwined. The warmth of his touch grounded her, reminding her that she wasn't alone in this journey anymore.

It's beautiful, isn't it? Emily said softly, her gaze fixed on the sky.

Michael nodded, his profile illuminated by the faint glow of the stars. It always has been. But tonight… it feels different.

Different how? she asked, tilting her head to look at him.

He turned to her, his blue eyes softening. Like we earned it. Like we fought for this peace.

Emily smiled faintly, leaning her head against his shoulder. We did.

They stood in companionable silence, the weight of everything they had endured finally easing. Emily's mind flickered back to the breach, to the way its energy had pulsed and shimmered, connected to every choice, every possibility. It had been terrifying and beautiful—a reflection of life itself.

What do we do now? she asked quietly.

Michael exhaled, the sound almost a laugh. Anything we want. The timeline's stable. SOLAR's gone. For once, we get to choose.

Emily considered his words, a spark of excitement flickering in her chest. After years of chasing answers, of being haunted by her father's legacy, the idea of forging her own path felt both exhilarating and terrifying.

I don't even know where to start, she admitted.

Michael smiled, brushing a strand of hair from her face. We'll figure it out. Together.

Her heart swelled at his words. Together. It wasn't just a promise—it was a lifeline. They had been thrown into chaos, tested in ways neither of them had expected, but they had come out stronger for it. Whatever lay ahead, she knew they could face it.

As they made their way back inside the observatory, the faint hum of the telescope filled the quiet space. Emily paused by the massive instrument, her fingers trailing along its cool metal surface.

My dad used to say the stars held the answers to everything, she murmured. That if you looked hard enough, you could find your place in the universe.

Michael leaned against the telescope, his gaze soft. Do you think he was right?

Emily thought about the breach, about the shimmering web of timelines and the choices that had led her here. She thought about her father's voice, his steady hands, and the way he had always encouraged her to dream big.

I think he was, she said, her voice firm. And I think we just found ours.

They left the observatory hand in hand, stepping into a world that felt new despite its familiarity. The night air was cool and crisp, the stars above brighter than Emily had ever seen them.

Emily, Michael said suddenly, stopping in his tracks.

She turned to him, her heart skipping a beat at the intensity in his expression. What is it?

Michael hesitated, then smiled softly. I just... I'm proud of you. For everything. For not giving up.

Her breath caught, warmth spreading through her chest. I couldn't have done it without you.

Yes, you could have, he said, his voice filled with quiet conviction. But I'm glad you didn't have to.

Emily's lips curved into a smile, and before she could respond, Michael leaned in, his forehead resting against hers. The moment stretched, quiet and infinite, like the time between stars.

We make a good team, he murmured.

The best, she whispered back.

The world hadn't changed overnight, but something fundamental had shifted. The breach was closed, the timeline was stable, and Emily had finally found peace—not in the answers she had chased, but in the connections she had forged.

As she and Michael walked away from the observatory, the stars above seemed brighter, closer, as if they were watching over her. The time between stars wasn't empty, she realized. It was full of possibility.

And for the first time, Emily wasn't afraid to embrace it.

The End.

www.ingramcontent.com/pod-product-compliance
Lightning Source LLC
LaVergne TN
LVHW050644200726
843506LV00010B/1359